true
ghosts
3

About the Author

David Godwin (Lakeville, MN) is the managing editor of *FATE* Magazine. He holds a Bachelor of Journalism degree from the University of Texas at Austin and is a student of esoteric lore, magic, and the Cabala.

To Write to the Author

If you wish to contact the author or would like more information about this book, please write to the author in care of Llewellyn Worldwide Ltd. and we will forward your request. Both the author and publisher appreciate hearing from you and learning of your enjoyment of this book and how it has helped you. Llewellyn Worldwide Ltd. cannot guarantee that every letter written to the author can be answered, but all will be forwarded. Please write to:

David Godwin
℅ Llewellyn Worldwide
2143 Wooddale Drive
Woodbury, MN 55125-2989

Please enclose a self-addressed stamped envelope for reply, or $1.00 to cover costs. If outside the U.S.A., enclose an international postal reply coupon.

true ghosts 3

even more chilling tales from the vaults of FATE magazine

unearthed and edited by
DAVID GODWIN

Llewellyn Publications
Woodbury, Minnesota

FIRST EDITION
First Printing, 2011

Based on book design by Steffani Sawyer
Cover art: Girl image © iStockphoto.com/Duncan Walker and the bare
     trees image © James Lazos/SuperStock
Cover design by Ellen Lawson
Editing by Ed Day

Library of Congress Cataloging-in-Publication Data
True ghosts 3 : even more chilling tales from the vaults of FATE Magazine
/ unearthed and edited by David Godwin.—1st ed.
     p. cm.
  ISBN 978-0-7387-2587-1
1. Ghosts. I. Godwin, David. II. Fate (Chicago, Ill.) III. Title: True ghosts
three.
  BF1461.T78 2011
  133.1—dc22
                                    2011011834

Llewellyn Publications
A Division of Llewellyn Worldwide Ltd.
2143 Wooddale Drive
Woodbury, MN 55125-2989
www.llewellyn.com

Other books by David Godwin

True Ghosts 2: More Haunting Tales from the Vaults of FATE Magazine

Light in Extension: Greek Magic from Homer to Modern Times

Godwin's Cabalistic Encyclopedia: Complete Guidance to Both Practical and Esoteric Applications

Contents

Acknowledgements

A heartfelt thank you goes out to Kyle B. Morton, *FATE* editorial assistant, for his work on this project. I would also like to acknowledge the invaluable assistance of Amber Petrik and Chris Mattox in the preparation of this manuscript.

Introduction

What would you do if you saw a ghost? Would you be
too frightened to move or would you be driven mad as
you behold something as unique as the presence of the
suddenly materialized dead? What would anyone really
do in that unexpected situation? While we cannot truly
train ourselves in the same ways that we prepare for flat
tires and delivering first aid, there is a place in the back
of our minds that is always expecting the unexpected.
The way I see it, having a paranormal encounter like
seeing a ghost is kind of like winning the creepiest lot-
tery imaginable. Because whether you consider it luck or
not, that person who sees a ghost is never going to forget
the experience for as long as they live (and probably as

a ghost too). And of course, not everyone gets to have the frightening joy of seeing a ghost or apparition, but for the ones who do; the telling and retelling of the story is as necessary as having experienced it to begin with. And for those of us who have never seen a ghost, we get to live vicariously through the printed text recounting the shared experiences of fellow readers that have had a glimpse of the great unknown and imagine what it must be like.

It's those recollections and tales gathered throughout the centuries and collected by *FATE* magazine that stimulate the mind and set our skin crawling. As the reader, you enjoy the luxury of being able to close this ghostly tome at any moment, but the storyteller is trapped forever with the spooks and specters that make up the stories. And have we got a collection of ghost stories fit for the living and the dead. And I mean real ghost stories, not that computer-generated shock fluff that Hollywood has been splattering movie screens with around the world. Nope, no Japanese remakes or teenager-marketed flavor of the month stories here, just dozens of true accounts of ghostly encounters, time-bending vortexes, and divine guidance from beyond. Stories from eyewitnesses that felt so compelled to share their experiences that they will be remembered in the bookshelves of *FATE* readers forever. For many people, seeing an actual ghost, spook, or specter can be the most frightening thing they would never want to imagine. For some, the most exhilarating and unexpected paranormal phenomena ghostly haunting represents a challenge in the hunt for the elusive evidence of life after death. And while television may be able to reach a broader audience with prime-time reality shows of all manner of ghost hunting, nothing can compare to firsthand accounts of *FATE* readers that comprise this book of ghostly tales.

So from me to the readers out there waiting to sink their teeth into another compendium of true ghost stories from the pages of *FATE* magazine: sit back and relax with this third installment of *True Ghosts* and pay no attention to the strange sounds of creaking floor boards or whispering disembodied voices you only *think* you hear. Ignore those cold spots floating through your room and don't mind the dog barking at odd stain on the wall, because you are about to go in search of ghosts, and hopefully, like me, you will find them before they find you!

—*Kyle B. Morton*
Editorial Assistant, FATE Magazine

Ghostly Apparitions

Have you ever seen a ghost? That's how the conversation usually begins when someone has encountered something that defies explanation. Those floating mists that shouldn't be, those snaps of light glimpsed out of the corner of the eye, and the fleeting images of lives long gone. Those are the things that our psyche refuses to ignore and leaves us forever disturbed by what we saw. The ghostly apparition is the spectral bread and butter of the fearless ghost hunter or the most common occurrence experienced by the unfortunately haunted. The uncanny apparition of a human form appearing and disappearing at will and the clichéd "bump in the night" only sound tame when we are not alone in the darkness. But only when the imagination and our primal fear of the unknown collide at the shock of witnessing a ghost do we really understand that our universe is capable generating many strange things.

For anyone who's ever desired to see the specters of the great beyond, no greater tales of intrigue and shock can be found in these stories reprinted from the pages of *FATE*. From the return of loved ones eternally lost to the horror of war to faces appearing in fires, we are compelled to believe that someone or something is attempting to make its presence known from beyond the grave. The classic tales of human forms glimpsed like a snapshot out of time seem as if human beings are capable of generating an energy that leaves a shadow stretching from the past to the present. Those are the tales of this chapter, those visceral accounts of ghostly images torn from the pages of *FATE* magazine resurrected here for scrutinizing eyes of the reader who will be the ultimate judge.

A Living Apparition

We had moved to Butler, Pennsylvania, in early March of 1957.

Our house was not really large enough for our family of nine children; nonetheless, when my husband's mother, Mrs. J. M. Johnson, became ill that same month, we moved her the 100 miles from her home to ours in an ambulance so we could take care of her. Because the house was small, we put up a hospital bed in our good living room, downstairs.

My kitchen was between the good living room and our family room. Early in April, I was quilting in the family room when my eyes were drawn suddenly to the door to the kitchen. There, framed in the doorway, I saw an apparition of my mother-in-law. I thought my eyes were playing tricks so I looked away. But when I looked back again the figure was still there. I sat and stared and, as I watched it slowly disappeared.

I knew from this she would be leaving us. I don't know why I thought she would die. I just felt she was telling me she was leaving.

Of course, I went to her bed immediately, but she seemed just as usual.

Nevertheless, I told my husband he should get her check cashed and pay her monthly bills.

He asked, "Why?"

I told him what I had seen and that I knew this meant she would be leaving us.

Two days later, on April 5, 1957, four months before her 73rd birthday, she died.

—*Catherine Johnson, Uniontown, Pa.*

Light in My Life

Since the fall of 1962, whenever I lie on my bed in the dark I see a light, a steady silvery glow high on my wall, always in the same place! It is only in my own bedroom when I am fully awake that I see these glowing, flame-like lights. Nothing else, odd or strange in nature, ever accompanies these lights.

I live alone with my various pets in a modest five-room home in a rural community of Azusa, California. North of our ordinary neighborhood are mountains with their ever-changing colors. To my knowledge, my 25-year-old rented dwelling has no history of violence or mysticism. During the several years of my tenancy when relatives have lived with me here, I never have seen the mysterious lights.

My mental state when I see these lights is one of peace and tranquility. They appear while I am praying, musing, or thinking of nothing in particular.

The light shows clearly very late at night or in the early morning hours on a bare plaster wall in a pitch-dark room. About the size of a quarter or a bit larger, the light glows eerily. Sometimes it dies abruptly as if a flashlight suddenly was flicked off. At other times, it seems to consume itself and burn out! Sometimes, almost as soon as I discover the light, it goes off as though embarrassed at being seen. Often, for months I never see this light.

Of course, I have looked for a natural explanation such as a passing car's headlights or a streetlamp. But I have discarded these and other possibilities. My bedroom wall, where the light appears, is devoid of pictures, and my window shades are always tightly drawn.

One night I awoke at 3:00 a.m. and my gaze immediately was directed to the bare wall behind my head. I saw a light similar to a candle flame glowing on the wall. I felt that I had been awakened for the sole purpose of viewing it. The light soon was joined by another candle flame, slightly higher up. They both glowed vividly. I went into the bathroom thinking, "When I return, the lights will be gone and that will be that."

But there they still were, in that very dark room just above the head of my bed on a level with my eyes, two lovely candle flames! They wavered as candles do. I put my hand over the lights experimentally, but this did not blot out their glow nor affect them in any way. Eventually, the "flames" died out, first one, then the other.

The last few times I saw a light on my wall it was a glowing pinkish streak shooting out like a falling star. From the first, I was deeply impressed that the light is not an "it" or a "thing" but that a wonderful personality is involved. I feel so happy afterward! When weeks go by without seeing the lights, I feel unexplainably sad.

With little changes in their manifestations, my lights continue, wonderful and erratic, vividly glowing on my bedroom wall.

—*Patricia Ellingson, Azusa, Calif.*

The Woman in Black

The Woman in Black has been my friend ever since 1932, when I first met her at the Mines Hospital in Tonopah, Nevada. That spring I suddenly became ill, and an emergency operation was performed. As there was little hope for my recovery, I was put in the little front room reserved for critical cases. The "No Visitors" sign hung on my door.

I was unaware of my surroundings until the fourth morning. Then, through what seemed like layers and layers of cotton I heard the rustling of silken garments. I forced open my eyes. Between the foot of my bed and the wall there was an open space, and in this space there now was a woman.

The woman was dressed in old-fashioned clothes. The bodice clung to spare breasts, and the skirt fell to the floor in heavy folds. On her head she wore a mantilla of heavy chiffon. The rusty black of her entire costume stood out in bold relief against the white wall as she paced back and forth from one side of the room to the other.

I watched her, puzzled but unafraid. As the morning grew older, her steps became slower. When I raised my head from the pillow to ask her a question she stopped pacing and grasped the bars on the foot of the bed. Her gnarled brown hands tensed with great strength.

Her luminous black eyes, which dominated her wrinkled and sorrowful face, penetrated mine. I seemed to sink into those pools of darkness. When I tried to speak. I knew I would not be able to say the words crowding my tongue.

She placed a bony finger to her withered lips. Slowly, almost sadly, she shook her head, as though to say, "No." Then she turned and seemed to fade through the window into the morning light beyond.

For some time afterward I lay wondering about her, her appearance and her gestures. A feeling of peace and strength slowly came to me. I became aware of life all about me, and summoning strength, I rang for Ellen Smith, the nurse.

Ellen showed surprise when she saw I was wide awake, but immediately busied herself straightening my sheet, turning the pillow, and pouring fresh water. At my persistent questioning about the strange woman, however, a fleeting expression of fright crossed her face.

After what seemed an eternity she whispered, "Don't be afraid. Others have seen her, too."

"Why does she come?" I asked. "Who is she? What does she want? Is she real?"

"I don't know," the nurse answered. "Turn over and rest now. Your pulse and temperature are normal this morning." She smiled and left the room.

In subsequent years, in moments of dire stress or danger, the Woman in Black has appeared to me fleetingly. Sometimes she is in a dream of an old abandoned house. Sometimes I just hear the unmistakable rustle of silken garments as she passes by. And having been warned too many times, I believe I will not be afraid when she comes to me and nods, "Yes."

—*Marguerite A. Vassar, Phoenix, Ariz.*

English Lavender

When my mother, Valerie Pose, passed on in 1956, we were thousands of miles apart. After moving to the United States I never found the opportunity to return to Germany even when my father wrote that mother was incurably ill.

I cannot describe the heartache I experienced when I learned of Mother's death. She never had seen her grandchildren and now, of course, they never would be able to know her.

Exactly one year after my mother died, I awoke in the night from a deep sleep. I was able to recall a complete dream. This was very unusual for me because never before had I remembered more than a few fragments of any dream.

In this dream, my mother had stood over my bed and, without uttering a word, beckoned me to follow her. It was late at night and the rooms were in darkness. Without ever having been in my home, Mother led me to the stairway and up to the floor on which my children's bedrooms were situated. Very slowly, she stepped toward each sleeping child and touched them all on the head in turn.

I kept talking to her incessantly, introducing each child. Even while I related small episodes in their young lives that I believed would interest her, I knew my mother was not alive and that what I was experiencing was a dream. After she had looked in on each grandchild, Mother turned and silently led me back down the stairs.

I did not want to let her go. There was so much I wished to tell her and never had the chance while she was alive. Just to keep her with me for a while longer, I asked my mother to have coffee with me. She declined, but motioned for me to help myself.

I don't remember how long I talked or what I talked about, but I remember her sitting across from me, nodding and shaking her head, sometimes looking puzzled, but listening intently without saying a word. Suddenly I found myself standing beside my bed and I knew my mother had left me.

While recalling my dream, I noticed a fragrance in my room. The scent was familiar to me. It became stronger until the odor became so intense I had to open a window. At that moment I realized that I was smelling English Lavender, my mother's perfume!

Although I never have used it myself, when I was a child, Mother used English Lavender generously every day. Hours later my bedroom was still filled with her fragrance.

I know that my mother did not come to me in a dream, for a dream does not leave a scent behind.

—*Erika Coppinger, Bay City, Mich.*

They Came Back

Since childhood I have seen the specter of dead persons, both those I have loved and those I have barely known. Two incidents are especially striking.

When I was six we lived in West Pittsfield, Massachusetts, near an icehouse where boxcars of ice were loaded for the railroad and packinghouses. I loved to sit around the platform and watch the icemen slide and guide the heavy cakes of ice into the train cars. One of these men was Big John Rinko, a dark Ukrainian who lived nearby with his childless wife.

He took a liking to me, and many times I shared his noon lunch. Even though I did not like the heavy bread and spiced meat, I pretended for the sake of friendship, to enjoy the food from his lunch pail. After eating, he would roll a cigarette and, letting me draw a few choking puffs, would laugh, calling me "the little onion that would grow stronger."

Early in 1932, when the ice harvest was over, after a year or two of our association, John Rinko died at age 45. I remember crying bitterly over his death and over death itself. I think this was my first realization of the inevitability of death, and for several days I was feverish from the idea of my mother, father, sister and brother, not to mention myself, coming to the final conclusion of our lives.

In April, I was playing with my brother behind the empty bunkhouse where the icemen kept a fire and lunch tables for their off-hours comfort. The work of the season was over, and except for our family (my father was caretaker of the plant), no one was about. My brother and I banged away with empty cap pistols, orally creating the gunfire. I faced the window at the rear of the bunkhouse, my mind concerned only with Tom Mix, Buck Jones, and Buffalo Bill.

Suddenly I saw Big John Rinko in the window, smiling at me as he always had. He wore his usual heavy wool shirt and flat greasy cap. His dark face was beard-stubbled; his smile was broad and broken-toothed. His hand lifted, and he beckoned me. I shouted his name excitedly. I had forgotten he was dead. "Big John!" I yelled, running around to the bunkhouse door. I heard my brother saying, "What the heck are you talking about? He's dead."

I opened the door and saw John Rinko across the room, moving toward me as big and natural as life itself, but then my brother's words seemed to slap me across the face. "He's dead." It was the realization that he was dead, I think, that broke the vision, for even as my friend called "Little Onion," he faded into nothingness before me.

My brother came up to me, saying, "There's nothing, nobody here." And there wasn't anymore. But there was a strong smell of tobacco, spiced sandwiches, and sweaty wool. However, I suppose, that was to be expected from a building that had housed a generation of hundreds of relaxing workmen. Later, when I returned to the scene with my dog, Prince, he howled and moaned pitifully with a fear I never had known him to show.

Years later I knew an elderly Greek gentleman, at whom I used to nod and say, "Good morning." I saw him at least once a week in the First National supermarket, laboriously pushing his cart about, nodding to those he knew, and forever asking stockboys where such and-such an item was located. "I'm 92," he would apologize.

For a long time he was part of the Pittsfield scene, neatly dressed, wearing nose-pressure glasses attached by a black ribbon to his lapel. Then he dropped out of sight.

Two or three years later, in 1963, I saw him again doing a little morning shopping. I nodded and he said, "Good morning."

"Haven't seen you lately," I ventured, not ever having spoken much to the old gentleman before.

"I'm 92 years old a' can't be 'round forever." He smiled, parting the lined, clean-shaven skin of his face. He touched his velour hat with his odd salute and moved his cart away. I saw him stop and speak with an assistant manager.

Then, as I shopped, I commenced thinking. He had claimed two or three years ago that he was 92, so how could he be 92 now? Later I spoke to the assistant manager.

"I see the Old Greek back this morning, Joe. Ain't been around lately. How come he's still 92?"

"You mean old Gus Dionyios who used to run The Big Apple fruit place? Guy with the black-ribboned eye-piece?"

"Yeah, the guy you were talking to a while back."

"Haven't talked to anyone this morning but the wife and the frozen food manager. You sure?" He looked at me disbelievingly. "That Greek's been dead for three years."

—*Francis J. Sibolski, Pittsfield, Mass.*

There is Another Life

On the last night of February 1939, when I retired I was unable to fall asleep. I was nervous and restless, which was unusual, as I never have any difficulty falling asleep quickly. When I finally did manage to sleep, it was more like a series of light naps than a sound sleep.

I awoke from one of my "naps" with such a start that I sat straight up in bed. Standing at the foot of my bed, her arms stretched out toward me, was a very dear cousin of mine. I was unable to move, but in a moment or two controlled my voice enough to call her name. She immediately disappeared.

I glanced at the clock on my bedside table; it was 9:30 p.m. I dismissed my vision, chalking it up to my nervousness or a dream, and went back to sleep.

The next morning, I picked up the paper and sat down to read while I drank my coffee. Across the top of the paper were the big headlines: "Prominent Woman Suicides." It was my cousin!

When I could control the shaking of my hands enough to hold the paper, I read on to find that the time of her death had been set somewhere between 9 and 10 o'clock. My vision of her had come at 9:30!

She was president of the P.T.A. and had gone to the meeting on the previous evening but had returned to her home about 9 o'clock for some much-needed documents that she had forgotten to bring with her.

When she failed to return, some of the other P.T.A. members called the house and, failing to get an answer, went out there. The house was locked and dark, and further investigation found my cousin lying in the garage in a pool of blood. She had shot herself in the head.

I have told the story of her appearance to me to several people. They all think I was dreaming. I now reject this idea—the coincidence of such a dream and the actual death of this same cousin at the same time is too great. I think I was sitting up in bed, wide-awake, and I feel that my cousin was trying to tell me something. What that something was, only eternity will reveal.

—Mary Hammond, Union City, Pa.

Penetrating Key

Great Aunt Maggie owned a small hotel in southern Michigan. Her boarders were almost permanent residents, some of them having made their home with her and my uncle for years. They were like one big, happy family.

On July 24, 1915, one of her young boarders took an excursion trip on the Eastland, a Great Lakes steamer. He left his room key with my aunt so she could clean his room while he was gone. My aunt was an excellent housekeeper with an unvarying schedule; everything was cleaned, dusted, and changed at a certain time. And everything was going as usual.

She had her arms full of clean linen for his room as she approached his door. Then she happened to glance down the hall. There she saw the young man walking slowly toward her, dressed as he had been when he left. He smiled at her and reached out silently for the key she had been about to put in the door.

He put the key into the lock, but it fell to the floor—inside the room!

And before Aunt Maggie could say a word, the dapper young man had vanished.

The door still was locked. My aunt was so astonished she dropped the linen and fled at top speed down the stairs. When she told my uncle and the others what had happened, they would not take her seriously. They just laughed.

It was quite a few minutes before she could convince them something was wrong. They followed her back up the stairs and down the hall to the boarder's room. Everything was as she had left it; the door was locked and the linen lay where it had fallen. There was no sign of the young man or of the key.

My uncle and another boarder tried to slide a paper beneath the door to see if my aunt had tried to play a joke on them by slipping the key under the door. But the paper would not pass under the door. There was no room.

Then my aunt remembered there was another key that might open the door. She brought it, but it did not work. There was nothing left to do but remove the door casing. That is what they did.

When the door was opened they found the key on the floor inside the room.

My aunt was sure something had happened to the young man and that it had been his ghost she had seen. It was only a little while later that word came that the excursion boat had capsized in the Chicago River. Hundreds had died, and one of the casualties was my aunt's young boarder.

—E. L. Swider, Marne, Mich.

Apparition at a Movie

When I was about 11 years old, my grandmother and I usually went to the movies on Saturday nights. While we were watching a movie on February 14, 1955, I heard my grandmother gasp and saw that she had turned pale. But since she said nothing to me and the movie was just beginning, I waited until we were on our way out of the theater, two hours later, to ask her what the trouble was.

She replied, "My Aunt Bel who lives down in Texas has died. I know because I saw her come into the theater and sit down in a seat three rows in front of us. She turned her face toward me for a moment. She looked just like she did the last time I saw her. She was visible only for about three seconds, then she disappeared."

We walked home in silence, wondering about this apparition.

Later that night a telegram arrived saying that Aunt Bel had died at 4:45 p.m.

Grandmother had seen her in the theater at about 7:00 p.m.

—*Lorraine Dudzik, Rosebud, Mo.*

Death's Farewell

About the turn of the century, my grandfather John Martin, was living in Princeton, Kentucky, with his wife and family. Because of his work and family responsibilities he had been unable to visit his parents and brothers and sister in Missouri since his marriage some years earlier. Communication not being as simple and fast as it is today, they seldom heard from each other.

One night as he lay in bed and just before sleep overtook him, John had a vision concerning his younger brother, Waller, who was living in Missouri at the time. In the vision, Waller came to see him. My grandfather looked out his window and saw the figure of a man walking down the road past his house. The man turned toward the window of John's bedroom and waved. When he turned, John saw his face distinctly in the moonlight. It was his brother! As Waller waved, John heard a voice that he instantly recognized as his brother's call out, "John, I just came to say goodbye." With that he disappeared.

A week later John received a letter from his parents, saying that Waller had died August 5, 1908, at Alton, Mo., of typhoid fever. It was the very night that John had had the vision! John replied to his family, saying, "Yes, I know that Waller died. He stopped by to bid me farewell!"

—*Patsy Killebrew, Hopkinsville, Ky.*

A Swatch of Chestnut Hair

Almost 60 years ago when we were living in Seattle, we had a wonderful friend and neighbor Mrs. Burns. She had an Ouija board and loved to tell fortunes, and many of her predictions actually came true. Even my sister and I, though only children, knew she was a mystical person, and above all, we loved to hear her tell ghost stories. Many of them Mrs. Burns claimed were true.

Mrs. Burn's daughter and my older sister were the same age and naturally became good friends as we grew up. When Veronica suddenly passed away at the age of 22, having been widowed in the meantime, she left a small daughter in a condition of severe need—both for care and money. Veronica had beautiful chestnut-colored hair and my sister agreed with Mrs. Burns that to sell a long swatch of it would bring in some money for the orphaned child—human hair being much in demand in 1906, as it is today.

The swatch was cut and formed and my sister temporarily placed it in a bureau drawer in the upstairs bedroom of our big old-fashioned house. One night I awakened suddenly, sensing a presence in the room. I sat up in bed but hesitated to get up to turn on a light. As my eyes became accustomed to the darkness I discerned a form moving slowly through the open door, across the room toward the bureau that held the swatch. All I could see was a pale figure wearing a long white gown. No moonlight or starlight nor streetlight came into the room, for the window shade was drawn. Thus the pale light had to emanate from the figure itself. As it drew closer, I recognized Mrs. Burns' daughter Veronica, her pale face wearing a natural but detached and peaceful expression. She moved directly to the bureau drawer. I was now too frozen to move, but I began to scream hysterically, clutching the blanket to my face as if to hide behind it. My mother, father, and sister frantically burst into the room, switching on the light as they came in. Now nothing unusual was to be seen. As I incoherently tried to explain the vision and my screams, we looked at the bureau and saw that the drawer was closed. My sister opened it and found the satin case in which she had stored the hair. It was lying open, its strings untied, although the hair itself was still there. My sister swore she had stored the case rolled up and neatly tied. But she doubted my story.

Only one person really believed me, I felt, and that was Mrs. Burns. When I told her my experience, she nodded wisely and said, "Many strange things happen, dear, that we can't explain but if we can't believe our senses, how can we believe anything?"

—*Erdeane M. Foster, San Bernardino, Calif.*

Can They Really?

"I wonder if they really can," mused Mother.

"If who can what?" I asked.

"One hears so much about dead persons returning as spirits, but can they really come back?"

A scary ghost story we were reading had set her off. I didn't try to answer her question.

It was 1944 in Berlin. Several heavy bombings a day had taught us to mean it when we said goodbye. My father had been killed in an air raid in November 1943, and we all lived under the constant threat of death. In a giddy mood one day in November 1944, Mother and I promised each other that the one to "go first" would return if it could be done without frightening the survivor. We both survived World War II, but life in the aftermath was not easy. The daily struggle made us forget our promise—or at any rate we stopped talking about it.

In 1947, Mother became ill and underwent surgery for a breast cancer. She recovered, but two years later the grim disease returned, and in January 1951, it took her life. The last time I saw Mother, she was in agony but still lucid enough to say, "I'm going to join Papa and you must go home now." I obeyed her. She died that night.

A few weeks later, I again heard Mother's agonized breathing. Thinking it was only a reflection of my grief I dismissed it. But the breathing sounds returned a little later and this time I saw my mother standing quietly in a corner of my bedroom, wearing her old black coat and narrow-brimmed black hat. She did not speak. Her repeated appearances over the ensuing years taught me that she made her presence known only when something important was about to happen to me.

In the next 10 years I moved 16 times, immigrated to Canada, then to the United States. In 1954 in Detroit, Michigan, I married and bore three children in the years between 1958 and 1963. Shortly after we settled in California, I fell mortally ill. In 1964 a doctor diagnosed my condition as a form of anemia that would kill me within two months. He told my husband to hire a housekeeper and to make funeral arrangements. Instead, my husband took me to the Loma Linda Clinic where a team of 12 physicians determined that I merely have an advanced case of pernicious anemia. While I am not physically strong, the disease is in control and I need not live in fear of my life.

A day or so ahead of every single one of these events —every move, my marriage, every birth, every consultation with physicians over my own condition—Mother appeared to me, as if standing by to do what she could.

Finally, a year ago, I tried to communicate with her. I asked her if she wanted to rest now. She answered me with an audible sigh as if pleased to be released from her promise.

A few days later both she and my father appeared to me. I saw them in an orange-colored aura without visible boundaries. Although they did not speak, they conveyed to me in some indefinable manner their state of well-being and happiness. They have not reappeared.

—*Brigitte Judd, Yucaipa, Calif.*

Where Did the Cider Go?

About 10 years ago, we lived on a road called Bingham Avenue near Poole in Dorset, England. Don Richardson was an acquaintance I saw at infrequent intervals. We didn't have much in common, but were quite friendly. Don was a peculiar fellow, an "unknown quantity," so to speak, and no one ever really got down to what he really thought about things.

One day he made one of his rare visits. My wife had gone shopping, and I looked forward to finishing up some odd jobs around the house. About 11:30 a.m. the door-bell rang. I cursed inwardly, as I wanted to get on with my work. The maid let him in and announced, "Mr. Don Richardson to see you."

I welcomed him, and we sat down to chat. After a time he said, "Well, I must be off. I have undertaken a long trip and you may not be seeing me again."

I inquired about his venture, but he was more than usually evasive. Some private business, I gathered, so I didn't pursue the subject. He rose to go.

"Come and have a drink," I said. "What's it going to be, beer or cider?" He chose cider, and I poured a generous glass for each of us and we drank. After a little more talk he said he had to be on his way. We shook hands and the maid saw him out.

Some days later I mentioned to another friend that I had seen Don Richardson and that we both liked cider.

My friend asked, "Are you absolutely sure he paid you a visit?"

I replied there was no mistaking Don anywhere or anytime.

Then my friend gave me a jolt. "I know you are a truthful person," he said, "and not given to daydreaming. But there's something mysterious here. Don Richardson has been dead for three months."

This made me feel quite odd. I am positive that Don did call; the maid had let him in and she had seen him out. When my wife returned from shopping she saw the two empty glasses on the sideboard. Just where did that cider go?

—J. P. J. Chapman, Poole, Dorset, England

Messages from the Dead

The dead have something important to say to the living and they will not be ignored. And in a world connected by a massive web of communications technology, sometimes the "old fashioned" ways communication can be just as effective as our electronic devices. Spirits dwelling in the afterlife may not have access to Facebook, but they still find ways to get in touch with the people. The reasons for these spectral messages can be as diverse as the ways in which they manifest. It could be as simple as some unfinished business that the departed must resolve before moving on or as important as advice meant to protect their descendants from harm. And while the dead find ways conversing with us, the living have also made their forays into communicating with the great beyond. In almost every toy store in the world, the simple game of Ouija can be found, and while most consider it harmless frivolity of youth, many regard the board as a gateway to the spirit world. Psychics, crystal balls, and séances remain the most popular ways to contact the dead, and while the results can at times be sketchy, it's the desire of the soul to reach out to those who have moved on to garner information from a truly unique perspective.

And yet, true rapport with the dead has remained elusive despite our best technological advances and our unwavering faith in spiritual modes of contacting the dead. Communication with the dead has been both a hallmark of many religions as well as a business for many a practitioner of the arts of divination. And so *FATE* proudly presents tales of the afterlife attempting to engage the living, some of which are as beautiful as they are bizarre.

Stroke of Death

Mother had lived all her married life in the house in Kanosh, Utah, to which she came as a bride. There she raised her large family and there, now, she was dying. For eight years she had been fighting a slow-growing cancer. Bedridden during her last year, 1937, we, her children, took turns taking care of her.

She was suffering horribly the night I came to care for her. Each night when I arrived I was in the habit of kneeling beside her bed and asking God to help her get well and live, but this night it was unbearable. For the first time, I changed my prayer, "Oh God, stop her suffering. No matter what it is going to cost us in grief and loneliness, please God, give her rest."

I rose and went into the other room, feeling guilty now that I had uttered those words. Had I been right to ask God to take any method to stop her suffering? Yet I could hear her moaning in pain from the bedroom, but had to wait 15 minutes before I could give her another injection, which would ease her pain only temporarily.

Just then my sister came in saving, "There is the funniest black cloud climbing up in the sky. If this were tornado country I would say it was a twister, but it must be a thunderstorm."

Suddenly the lightning flashed. We both ran for Mother's room and as we threw open the door the whole room seemed momentarily wrapped in fire. It gradually died out, but the house shook from the loud crash of thunder that had accompanied it.

We looked at Mother. She seemed dead, but when we reached her bed we realized she was still breathing, but unconscious. As we carried her from the room, which had a "strange burnt smell," I wondered whether Mother had been struck by lightning, or if the fear had been too much for her.

We laid her on the spare bed and began to strip off her clothes, which also had that strange smell. Suddenly we saw the clothing was full of tiny holes no larger than the head of a pin. Frightened, we called the doctor, who came immediately. He examined her and discovered the holes were all over her body as well, but he could give no explanation for them.

After the doctor left, my sister and I noticed the storm had passed. And then we realized that there had been only one stroke of lightning!

For the next three days Mother lay in a coma. Late on the third night, my sister and I were sitting in the kitchen having coffee. We were fearful of losing Mother and we trying to convince ourselves it was for the best. Yet, we could not help feeling guilty at our relief that Mother was suffering no longer.

Just then we hear a frightening noise, like crushing, grinding glass. As it became louder and louder, we rushed to Mother's room. As soon as we reached the door, the noise stopped and instead we heard Mother calmly talking to someone. At last we recognized the other voice. It was our dead aunt's! We stood there entranced, until finally we came to our senses and jerked open the door, expecting to see Mother wide awake and rational. But there she lay, smiling and calm in death.

—*Etta Slaughter, as told to Velma Dorrity Cloward, Modesto, Calif.*

A Tail of Ouija

The subconscious is blamed for a lot of strange phenomena, but I'm willing to bet it can't pull all the tail feathers from a parakeet!

It has been said that the subconscious actually makes a Ouija board work, but I doubt it, especially after an experience my 17-year-old daughter Pat and I had.

The two of us had been getting some surprisingly correct answers questions about things we could not possibly have known. One night, January 19, 1962, just for fun, we asked Ouija if he could prove he was in the house. The time was 9:00 p.m.

Ouija answered, "Yes," and said to shut the bedroom door. He could prove it.

In the bedroom, Pat's pet parakeet sat perkily in his wire cage on dresser, where he had lived for over a year. The gate on his cage was tied securely to make sure he did not escape and fly outdoors, as the bird before him had done.

We shut the bedroom door and waited.

We had not waited long when we heard the parakeet screech. By the time my husband, daughter, and I opened the door, the chattering commotion in the bedroom had ceased.

The bird was not in his cage, but was quivering under the bed. On the rug were all his tail feathers. The door of his cage was still tied, and he could not have squeezed between any of the wires. He never had got out before, and he never got out again.

How did he get out this time? And who or what pulled out his tail feathers? I cannot explain it, but I certainly will not blame it on the subconscious!

—*Mildred Lindley, Salinas, Calif.*

A Promise Kept

I learned to tell fortunes with cards simply for its entertainment value. One evening in 1935, in Santa Cruz, California, my hostess at a party asked me to read the cards. She knew I foretell only happy events and do not make morbid predictions.

Therefore, I was astonished to see Mr. Shortridge become angry when I said he was considering a new position but that he wouldn't go through with it.

"Why not?" he asked.

I answered, "You'll change your mind."

His face grew red and he and his wife soon left our party.

However, to my surprise Mr. and Mrs. Shortridge appeared at my home the next morning. He said he was bothered by what I had seen for him in the cards. Although he appeared embarrassed he asked me to "run the cards" again.

Dropping my work I tried to reassure him saying, "They are only cards. Don't let them upset you."

Then, try as I might, I couldn't see anything in the cards for Mr. Shortridge. We began discussing occult experiences and somehow I became inspired to talk, as I never had talked before, about my reasons for believing in life after death.

Mr. Shortridge regarded me strangely and said he never before had heard such ideas expressed. He didn't believe in life after death, he said. When a person dies "that ends it for keeps," he insisted. "But," he went on, "if I died and could come to you I'd do it, to show you you are right. You deserve it!"

A week later, while I was busy in my kitchen one morning, I looked up to see Mr. Shortridge smiling at me. I seemed to be seeing him through a curtain. I called, "Oh, Mr. Shortridge, I see you!"

I was very excited. I never before had seen an apparition, and I never have seen one since.

When my husband returned from work in the evening I rushed to tell him what I had seen.

"That's odd," he exclaimed. "Mr. Shortridge died this morning of a heart attack. It happened about the time you say you saw him in spirit."

This experience has given me comfort all my life. I truly believed in what I had told Mr. Shortride before this wonderful experience, but Mr. Shortridge in keeping his promise to me proved beyond all doubt that we do live after the change called death.

—Mae Esty Morgan, Santa Cruz, Calif.

Matthew's Moose

Matthew is a young Eskimo man living on the Yukon River in a small Eskimo settlement, Mt. Village, in Alaska. His father once was the best hunter in the village, or for that matter, in the whole area. He provided well for his large family of sons and daughters and always had gifts of meat for less fortunate families in the village. The Shaman, an old man when I first knew him, depended upon him for most of his winter's meat. None of his sons were good hunters. They had no need to be; their father always had provided for them. But then Matthew's father, the great hunter, died.

Winter was coming on and there was little food in Matthew's house. Matthew was growing desperate. He knew, as the oldest son, it was his duty to provide for his family. Perhaps he could have faced starvation for himself, but not for his family. He felt, too, that the other men in the village looked at him with less respect now. He could not stand the shame.

On a particular night he lay sleepless, knowing something must be done soon—but what? Then there was a scratching on the door. Softly, yet insistently, it came. Matthew slipped quietly from beside his sleeping family and went outside.

A fur-clad figure outside the door wordlessly beckoned him to follow and led the way to the *kashim*—the men's bathhouse. In the light of the moon, he recognized the fur-clad figure as the old Shaman and his knees shook as he realized something very important must be about to happen.

"My son, I respected your father above all men in the village. He provided me with much meat and was kind to the others in the village. Now he is worried because he did not teach his sons to be good hunters. I don't want him to be unhappy in the other world. It should not be so," the old Shaman said. They were standing in the kashim now with the moonlight shining through the smoke hole in the roof.

"I do not go along with the white man's laws about hunting seasons. Eskimos take meat when they need it. They don't take it when they don't need it, as the white man often does. But, so that you will know when it is the right time, we will observe the white man's law. On the first day of hunting season for moose, you will go alone and very early to the sand point across the river from the village. A fine big moose will be standing there at the edge of the willows. You will shoot him. You will not miss. You will have plenty of salmon, and this should provide your family with enough meat."

And now Matthew suddenly found himself alone in the kashim. It was as if the Shaman never had been there. But he knew that he had, for had he not given detailed instructions? Matthew walked many hours that night before he could go home and sleep. Then he slept soundly and woke refreshed. Minutes after he awoke, the house was a babble of excited voices. The old Shaman had been found dead in his bed—I was present when he was found. He had died in his sleep. The village mourned him and Matthew mourned with them, and wondered to himself.

When the moose season opened, Matthew went, as the Shaman had instructed, to the point across the river from the village. Sure enough—there was a fine moose. He got it with the first shot. He did not miss.

That was a number of years ago and, to this day, Matthew gets his moose each year on that point. Missionaries, the priest, the schoolteacher, and traders in the area tell me Matthew always seems to get his moose on the first day of the season. Others say they have hunted in this same area without seeing a sign of moose.

I first knew Matthew in 1955, and it was perhaps 1959 when he told me this story of his successes as a hunter.

—*Nan Hampton, Barrow, Alaska*

Last "Goodbye"

When we were young our father never would allow us to say "Goodbye" to anyone unless we were sure we never would see this person again.

In 1914 I was working on a small cattle ranch about 75 miles from Charleyville in Queensland, Australia. About five times a year, my father, a state policeman in the district, would drop in to see me. I had been at the ranch for three years when he visited me on my 17th birthday.

He spent half a day with me; then, as usual, I rode with him halfway to the temporary police station. Then we would part, each with about 10 miles to ride.

As we parted on this particular day, impulsively I blurted, "Goodbye, Dad." He just looked hard at me, then said, "I will see you again."

Three months later I was preparing camp at a water hole, when some strange compulsion caused me to step away from the light of my campfire. Standing in the open glade in his mounted police uniform was my father. I had started to walk toward him when he waved his hand and said, "Goodbye, lad."

Then he faded away. I rode back to the ranch, where the owner met me with a telegram informing me that my father had died 300 miles away, after being thrown from a horse.

—*George J. Gale, Olympia, Wash.*

Talk with a Dead Aunt

I talked with my aunt for about 15 minutes. If you think there is nothing strange about this, let me tell you that my aunt has been dead for over 50 years.

This occurred in 1963, and my aunt has not reappeared. At the time, I was a religious lay brother living in a monastery in Nebraska. My duties were to keep the monastery in running order. I took care of the gardens and grounds and also helped in the laundry room. Every evening after my work was finished I would visit the chapel and kneel before the altar to pray. At these times, I would pray for my fellow brothers, priests, my family, and all my deceased relatives.

After about a year of this routine daily, I felt a strong urge to pray for and to my Aunt Alice, my mother's sister who died soon after birth. I felt that the baby, Alice, committed no sins—and I knew that Jesus loves the young and innocent—so I believed her to be a saint. Of course, this was my belief and not that of the order or the Catholic faith. In fact, no one knew that I was praying to my aunt.

One June night after a hot and sticky day, we had a severe thunderstorm. Unable to sleep, I visited the chapel, which is attached to the monastery. I knelt in the last pew and prayed that the monastery and all its inhabitants would be spared from any harm due to the storm. I implored the aid of my "saintly" aunt.

Suddenly I felt very cold. The wind from outside seemed to be rushing through the chapel. The chapel had been dark, except for flickering red votive lights that cast weird shadows on the walls, but now I noticed a light glowing by the communion rail. It was hazy, fuzzy, about the size of a baseball, and seemed to be throbbing.

I walked toward it as if compelled to do so. I spontaneously knelt in front of it.

"Dear God, what is this? What does it all mean?" I repeated these questions over and over while staring at the glowing light—almost hypnotically.

The mysterious light then descended. It rested on the chapel floor for a moment or two, then disappeared into the tile.

Still kneeling I felt the place beneath me shake. My mind seemed to spin and I felt myself going down … down through the floor … into the earth … I was cold. I was falling downward still in my kneeling position. All I could see before my eyes were blurry streaks. The coldness suddenly disappeared. I was comfortable … I stopped falling. I now knelt on cushion-like ground in a cave beautifully lighted and colored light blue. I could smell the fragrance of roses and still immediately before me was that mysterious light.

Quickly, I made the sign of the cross on my person. No sooner had I done so than this "light" began to grow … turning into a beautiful young girl about 16 to 18 years old.

She stared at me and smiled.

"Are you the Blessed Mother?" I asked.

Gently she shook her head. "I, dear Brother, am your Aunt Alice."

"But," I said in amazement, "You died while an infant. How come you … "

"How come I look the way I do?" she finished my question. "Well, when we die we all are judged by God. Those who lived a good life go to heaven and no matter at what age you die, one month or 100 years old, you will look like a young adult. There is no ugliness or disfigurement here. But Brother, be patient, I have important words for you.

"One of my sisters will die tomorrow … no, not your mother. It will be your Aunt Joyce. But I am now concerned about your mother. Joyce will be happy. But your mother is ill. Doctors think it is a stroke. They are wrong. It is multiple sclerosis. She is old. Your father is old. They both need you at home. God appreciates you giving your life for Him by your Brotherhood vocation, but He wants you home with them."

Before I could answer, the figure disappeared and I felt myself being pulled upward. Soon I was back in the chapel, kneeling at the communion rail as before. But now there was no light. A tremendous thunderclap echoed through the chapel following a particularly brilliant flash of lightning. The religious habit I was wearing was drenched with sweat. Shaking like a leaf, I went back to my cell. There I threw myself on my bed and just stared at the ceiling.

The next morning I was the first one in chapel. At the communion rail, I sheepishly looked for a hole in the floor. Of course, there was none.

Later that day as I was working in the garden, hoeing the flowers, Father Paul called out to me from the window. A telephone call.

Some minutes later, I hung up the phone and stood staring out the window. My Aunt Joyce was dead, just as the vision had predicted.

Now I am at home. I left my religious lay-brother vocation. I am with my mother and father. They are old and they need me. About a month ago the doctors at a famous New York hospital rediagnosed my mother's condition—she has multiple sclerosis!

—Barry Kosky, Staten Island, N.Y.

A Throbbing Message

Coming home from school on the evening of December 20, 1915, 13-year-old Dorothy Merens stopped at the cabin where her father's Negro tenants lived. While she was there visiting, they all suddenly heard a frightening sound that seemed to come from Dorothy's head. It was a deep, dull sound, as of something very heavy beating on flesh. *Thud! Thud! Thud!*

The Negroes fled screaming from the cabin, and Dorothy ran for home. She began calling as she neared the house and her stepmother came to the door. For several minutes Dorothy could only cry and sob while Mrs. Merens asked her over and over what was wrong.

When Dorothy finally managed to tell what she had heard down at the cabin her stepmother said, "That's impossible. You have lost your mind. Go lie down. I'm going down to the barn to get your father and Tom."

But she had barely gotten Dorothy down on the bed when the dreadful sound came again from right over her pillow. Mrs. Merens heard it herself, only too plainly. *Thud! Thud! Thud!* She ran screaming from the house, calling Mr. Merens as she ran. He rushed to meet her and when she gasped out the story he said, as Mrs. Merens herself had said only minutes before, "You have lost your mind."

He rushed to the house, where he found the terrified Dorothy sobbing wildly. He tried in vain to pacify her. And presently Mr. Merens himself heard that deep, hollow sound from over Dorothy's head. *Thud! Thud! Thud!* He was astounded. Now he was hearing things. As Dorothy was hysterical he called Dr. Walton.

Over the telephone, Dr. Walton was frankly skeptical. "Either you've all got head noises or somebody is ticktacking your house. Look around for wires?"

"I tell you it's nothing of the kind. It started down at the cabin. They couldn't ticktack both places. I want you to get out here and give Dorothy something to quiet her."

By the time the doctor arrived it was dark and the Merens' house was full of curious neighbors. Some of them had heard the ominous sounds, too, and their excited chatter was deafening.

Dr. Walton ordered out all the neighbors and asked Dorothy, "Don't you think you just might be pounding your chest yourself without realizing it?"

"No, no, no! I didn't! I didn't!" she wailed. "Make it stop!"

The doctor said, "All right. I'll give you some medicine and you'll go to sleep and forget it." He gave her a hypodermic and then put out the light. Seating himself beside the bed, he held his hands just above the girl's chest so that he would know if she made any movement.

Almost at once, the sounds began again. Dr. Walton was astonished. He knew there had been no movement at all. Dorothy cried out at first, but under the influence of the hypo, she gradually became calm and soon was asleep.

Dr. Walton turned on the light again and they all watched her. After a few minutes she began to talk, but it was not Dorothy's voice; it was the voice of her mother who had died eight years earlier. Mr. Merens looked frightened. He stared at the others. "That's Katy's voice. That's Katy," he repeated.

They heard the words distinctly. "Dorothy, tell your father that he and Tom must pay their debts. They must pay their debts." Then the girl was quiet.

Dorothy now slept peacefully the night through, but there was much whispering and shaking of heads among the neighbors. One woman said, "It must be that Dorothy is a medium and just didn't realize it. I guess poor Katy was trying all the time to get the message to her and this was the only way. Maybe her spirit will rest now."

Early the next morning the neighbors saw Mr. Merens and Tom driving their heavily loaded hay wagons toward Penelope, Texas. They knew that the men were taking the hay down to pay their debts at the stores and the lumberyard.

Dorothy and the family never heard those hollow frightening sounds again. Perhaps, as the neighbor had said, Katy Merens' troubled spirit was now at rest.

—*Ella Marie Farmer, Dilley, Tex.*

Finders Keepers!

One quiet afternoon in January this year, my friend Karen and I were playing with our Ouija board as we often do just for fun. As we sat thinking of what questions we might ask, the planchette (the guiding table on which one's fingers are placed in using the board) started to move, giving us its own message.

We were a little scared at first, but as it started spelling out the message we became too involved to be frightened!

Our communicator called herself "Meg," saying she was 19 years old and that she died in the year 1850, having lived in the Midwest. The message transmitted to us was this:

"Go and light the light in the attic. Go in front of house, face window, stand under the flag, pull the board; under the board you will find something lost 42 years ago."

I have lived in this Cleveland house for four years but have never had any reason for going to the attic. I've had nothing to store there, so I didn't even know there was a flag.

Excited by this time, we followed the instructions in the message. When we lifted the board in the musty attic's floor, we found a fifth of whiskey wrapped in a newspaper dated December 21, 1924. That made the bottle 42 years old.

Our friends used to laugh at us when we claimed to contact spirits through the Ouija board, but now they believe us. We have saved both the paper and the bottle to prove we received a message from another world.

—*Sandra Pappas, Cleveland, Ohio*

Unofficial Notification

During the last war, I was living in London and my husband was serving in France with the British infantry. Not receiving any mail from him for several days had made me quite uneasy.

One night as I lay sleepless in bed, the figure of my husband suddenly appeared to me. He was wearing army battle dress. He sat on the end of my bed, resting his head in his hands. I lay there too startled to move and he looked at me sadly. He said very distinctly, "Oh dear, oh dear!" and disappeared.

The next morning, filled with foreboding, I went to the Foreign Office in Whitehall where official casualty records at that time were kept. I asked one of the clerks if they had any news of my husband and gave him his name and number.

I watched the clerk eye the column of casualty figures from the previous day's fighting. Suddenly, his finger stopped halfway down the column and he looked at me with sympathy in his eyes.

Yes, my husband's name was on that list—"killed in action." The British government would have notified me the next day, but my husband chose to come back from the great unknown to communicate with me himself.

—*Violet Mack, Culver City, Calif.*

Fear of Death Undone

My father, Parley S. Checketts, despite his religious convictions and staunch faith in God, had a deep-rooted fear of death. As he grew older, he displayed a similar fear of hospitals, doctors, illness—anything that might take him away from his family.

His life always revolved around his family and his home. We lived in the same house in Ogden, Utah, for many years and as we grew up and married and left home we still remained close in spirit.

My brother Bob, my sister Betty, and I were all at home in 1935 when my father suffered a paralytic stroke. He had just passed his 50th birthday. The doctor immediately said that he would recover, but the stroke would leave him partially crippled and make speaking difficult.

Father adamantly refused to go to a hospital so Mother nursed him at home through long months of recovery. But as the doctor had said, he did get well—and he worked 20 years longer before retiring. Throughout those years, his speech impediment made him self-conscious and he disliked going anywhere without Mother or some member of the family.

His second stroke came in June 1956, shortly after he retired. I was working in the yard when Mother called me. She was very upset and weeping as she told me Dad seemed to be coming out of a brief unconsciousness, but he seemed bewildered and didn't know her.

When I reached my father, I was startled by the sheer terror in his eyes and the piteous whimpering sounds coming from his throat, like the sobs of a tiny baby in great pain. My emotions in turmoil, I sought some means of comforting him, some way to relieve the torture that made him writhe as he frantically clung to me.

I think I must have prayed silently—and suddenly a calm warm feeling enveloped me. I knew what I must say and the answers to questions I had asked all my life ran in panorama through my mind.

I placed my right hand on my father's forehead and started to speak in a low tone that didn't sound like my own voice.

"Dad, you must listen to me now. Can you hear me?"

He relaxed and the sobbing ceased. Sighing like a child who has been comforted after a nightmare, he nodded his head.

I told him he had had another stroke, and the doctor would come in a few minutes. I went on to say this was the beginning of the end, and these strokes would come again and again and any one of them might be the last. He must never again be afraid, for he never would be far from his family. When the final time came, he would just get up and walk out of the room into a grand and glorious freedom. Thinking of my brother Bob, who had died six months previously, I assured my father someone would meet him, someone he loved.

As I talked, a warm light of understanding overcame the terror-stricken expression in his eyes and he seemed to be more comfortable. When the doctor came, he confirmed our fear that it was another stroke.

Soon after this, my work took me to Santa Monica, California, and in my heart I knew I never again would see my father alive. A year passed and the strokes became more frequent, each time lasting longer, until he became helpless and bedridden. Despite his pleas, he had to be taken to a hospital, where he died on August 17, 1959. Mother told me he never again betrayed that awful terror until the last moment, when he seemed to be fighting the transition.

The news, though expected, was hard to take. I told my wife I wanted be alone for a little while and retired to my room. As I sat on the edge of my bed in the dark, once again I experienced that warm comfortable feeling as if I were not alone. Then I beheld a strange phenomenon. My room grew lighter and suddenly—it seemed so natural—father stood before me.

Still clad in a white hospital gown, his hair rumpled, he seemed breathless and excited. His eyes shone as he flexed his arms and extended his fingers. He looked at me and said, "Son, I had to come to tell you. Look at me! I can walk and I can talk clearly again. I feel free and I have no pain."

He paused and a look of disappointment came over his face. "You told me there would be someone to meet me," he said, his eyes roving over the room.

I told him not to be afraid and while I was speaking my brother Bob, who died in January 1956, in Phoenix, Arizona, walked into the soft golden light now suffusing the room.

He took Dad by the arm and said, "Would you like to come with me? We have a lot to do."

As they started to move away my father turned and put out his hand.

"Aren't you coming with us, Don?" he asked.

My brother shook his head and said, "Not yet, Dad. Don will join us later."

At that instant I felt I would give anything to go with them. Then they simply walked out of the room and the golden light faded.

In August 1962, my mother's death shocked us all. She had remained in her Ogden home visiting one or another of her children from time to time. She had not been ill and everyone remarked how well and happy she had been the day before she died.

I think I am the only person who knows what really happened. She had written me the week before that she was feeling at peace and in the best of health and that lately it seemed as if Dad were in the house with her. I believe he was and that she reached out and took his hand and they walked away together. I am just as sure that some day I too will take that walk to join them.

—*Don H. Checketts, Ogden, Utah*

Dream Visitations

Where do our dreams come from? Are dreams the result of our conscious and subconscious minds engaged in a contest of abstract problem solving? Or are dreams derived from a state of mind that provides access to the infinite energies flowing through the universe? The silent slumber of our most vulnerable state may also be the transcendental bridge between this life and the afterlife. The dreams that plague or enchant our sleep have long been considered greatly important messages of inspiration and foreboding. We desperately grasp at the images as the subconscious bends its will to the ether of world's unfathomed, giving rise to messages beyond space and time that defy logical explanations.

Often the visitations are meant to give guidance to the dreamer in the forms of warnings and glimpses of possible futures. People have reported the strange interjection of loved ones in familiar places engaging the dreamer with warnings to avert disaster or guide them on their journey through life. And sometimes we are visited by loved ones who wish to put our guilt-burdened consciences at ease.

The following stories are truly heartfelt and endearing, reminding us that our love and unwavering passion for our friends and family is capable of transcending death. And just as Hamlet haunted by the ghost of his father pondered to himself during his soliloquy, we must also wonder "for in that sleep of death what dreams may come when we have shuffled off this mortal coil must give us pause."

Conscience Pain

My sister Dora and her husband had five children, and times on their farm were very hard. They had bad luck with everything they tried to raise. The pretty tomatoes rotted in the fields, and other crops froze when there was an unprecedented early freeze.

Dora worked in a little cafe to help make ends meet. Her husband, Raymond, moved four old men who had pensions into the house to care for, but when the sandstorms got so bad that they covered the railroad tracks in front of their house, the old men packed up and left.

Sometimes I stopped to see them; sometimes I took them food when I knew they were hungry, and we helped out in other ways too, but I did none of these things often enough for a Christian woman who professed to love her sister. Many, many times after it was too late, I thought of the things I should have done.

Thanksgiving Day was Dora's birthday in 1958, so we had a family party at Dora's house. We invited all five sisters and their families, but only two came. We had enough food to last a week.

It was the last day that I spent with her. Many things kept me from getting over to see Dora, even though I knew she was not well. There was my daughter's new baby, the Christmas programs, and my own indifference. I even bought Dora a Christmas present, which she never got. I could not give her a present when I had none for her children. I had planned to buy them all something real nice, but my husband, who did not approve of Dora's husband, demurred, although we both knew full well they didn't receive any Christmas presents at all.

On Christmas Day, I heard that Dora was ill; still I made no effort to see her. But on January 4, I left my children at her home and she was happy to see them. When I picked them up again, after attending an anniversary party, I remember distinctly how translucent her face was when I kissed her goodnight. It was as if a light shone from it.

Two days later, on January 6, we were awakened by someone beating our door. It was Raymond, my brother-in-law, and Pat, one of their boys. I let them in.

They cried and screamed, "She is gone. My God, she's dead!"

They wanted me to go back home with them, but I wouldn't go. My husband went. I must have disappointed even my Maker. For I said as plain as day, "I'll go later."

Dora had died in bed, never even moved, just slept on. The day before she had cleaned her whole house and had felt exceptionally good, her family said. I will always feel that if I had helped her do her cleaning just once a week she would still be alive today. This is what my conscience tells me.

A year later, when things had gone from bad to worse with Dora's family, I took three of her children to live in our home. Susan went away to school and my sister, Emily, adopted Jane, and I had the other three. When friends praised me for doing this, it only hurt me for I was paying a debt of love I shouldn't have incurred. My conscience continued to torment me, day after day. For three years I prayed that God would forgive me for my neglect and indifference to my sister's plight. I felt that in order to be forgiven, I had to feel the forgiveness. But it didn't come.

Then one Sunday when I was alone in the kitchen, putting ice in the glasses for our Sunday dinner, I heard the door open. I turned to look and there was Dora, standing there. I was like one in a trance. I started to walk toward her and she vanished. I felt weak all over. I didn't tell the children, or my husband, who would have laughed at me.

But the next weekend my married daughter, who lives on a farm about 20 miles away, was home for a visit and she told me, "Mother, you know I saw Aunt Dora standing in my kitchen last Sunday about noon. I nearly fainted. She disappeared just like she came. What do you think about this?"

It all seemed unbelievable, but I knew it was true. The old hurt in my conscience was worse. I doubled my praying to God to forgive me, but of course I could not sit around and mope. It is not my way, and anyway a family of seven does not leave much time for idleness.

Last December, in 1962, we had a wonderful Christmas. They are all our children now, without distinction, and each one got something real nice. We had a big turkey dinner with all the trimmings and I know everyone enjoyed it.

Several nights after this, I had a dream. I dreamed that all seven of us—Dora's three children, and my two children who still live at home, my husband and I—were driving down the road in our white station wagon when a new green Ford pickup truck passed. I cried, "That is Dora, your mother!" Then we passed her again and she waved at us and gave us her happiest smile. We all waved back at her. I awoke with a start, to find the ache in my heart was all gone. The pain of my nagging conscience had left and in its place was the feeling of having been complimented by Dora.

—*Ruby H. Krueger, Encinal, Tex.*

I Waved Goodbye

When I was a child living in Hutchinson, Kansas, I often visited my maternal grandmother, Rachel Moore, who lived near us. My grandfather had died before my birth and I knew him only from photographs. In those days I often dreamed.

And because my dreams were so vivid, I usually related them to my family the next day. One morning I told this dream.

I had seen Grandpa come up the walk at Grandma's home, cross the porch, and go into the front parlor. Grandma came in from the kitchen, wiping her hands on her apron. She showed no surprise but motioned to his big chair.

"Sit down, William. I've been hoping you'd come," she said.

I ran into the garden to tell Aunt Lily. She came at once and joined her parents in the parlor.

"You have been gone so long, Papa. I hope you can stay with us now," Lily said in my dream.

"No. I came to get Rachel. I have missed her and want to take her back with me," Grandpa replied.

"Well then," Grandma said, moving toward the bedroom, "I must change my dress and comb my hair. I will not be long, William."

In this dream, I was sent to tell my mother and Uncle John that Grandpa was home and that he was taking Grandma away with him. By the time they returned with me, Grandma was ready. Everyone said goodbye and then my two grandparents crossed the porch hand-in-hand, down the walk to the front gate, and on out of sight.

At the end of my dream story my mother sat looking at me. She said nothing for a few minutes. Then she told me, "My dear, your grandma died last night. She has gone to heaven to be with Grandpa. Only Aunt Lily, Uncle John, and I were with her when she left us."

"Don't forget me. I was there too, to wave goodbye!" I protested.

—*Edna Beattie, San Jose, Calif.*

Urgent Message

Awoke from my dream with such a start that at first I thought my hand had come in contact with a live electrical circuit. In my dream my brother, Glenn, who had been dead for over a year, had come to me with a package instructing me to gift-wrap it and take it to our father as soon as possible. Glenn seemed aware of the fact that the recent difficult birth of my son had kept me from traveling 40 miles to see our ailing father, D. D. Smith, who lived in Philadelphia, Pennsylvania.

As my brother turned to go, I asked how he could visit me when he was dead. He reached out and touched my hand, imploring me not to be afraid. As our hands touched again an electrifying shock raced up my arm, instantly awakening me.

Two days later, on February 28, 1955, I went to see my father. I assured myself the dream had nothing to do with this sudden decision. I merely was anxious for my father to meet his new grandson, I told myself. However, I knew the dream was urging me on.

I found my father's health so improved that, on the way home, I sheepishly related the dream and its resultant fears to my husband. We both agreed that dreams were meaningless.

But the next day, March 1, we knew better. My sister called to tell me father had had a stroke and had died.

—*Phyllis R. Haag, Williamstown, N.J.*

The Telegram

My grandfather, Orman L. Kimbrough, usually chipper in the morning, this day walked slowly into the dining room for breakfast. As he took his place at the head of the table, I noticed he looked tired and worn.

"Didn't you sleep well, Orman?" asked my grandmother as she filled the children's plates.

Grandfather sighed and wearily passed a hand over his forehead.

"I was restless and dreamed about Caesar all night," he confessed. His half-brother Caesar lived in Texas, many miles from our Mississippi home.

He went on, "I dreamed that he was dead. I would wake up and then when I'd get back to sleep I would dream the same thing again, over and over. It bothers me. I'm worried about Caesar and I haven't heard from him for a long time."

"Oh, he's all right!" said Grandmother cheerily. "He's probably too busy to write. You'll hear soon."

We talked of other things for a few minutes and then the doorbell rang. When Grandmother came back into the dining room, she held a yellow envelope. She looked frightened as she handed it to Grandfather.

He hastily tore open the envelope, glanced at the message and cried hoarsely, "Caesar died last night!"

—*Louise B. Meek, Grenada, Miss.*

"Dreaming True"

I was living in Calverton Park, Missouri, in October 1959, when I had the strangest dream of my life.

As the dream began, I found myself in a limousine alone except for a chauffeur who slowly stopped the automobile at curbside. I waited patiently for something to happen—it seemed several minutes—and then the chauffeur told me to get out.

"Why? What is this place? What am I supposed to do?"

Without turning or letting me see his face the chauffeur said firmly, "I have brought you where you are supposed to be. You must get out."

I opened the car door and stepped out onto an ordinary city sidewalk, but I could see no buildings or houses. It was a pleasant sunny morning. Only when I looked down to see I was dressed entirely in black did the first twinges of apprehension strike. I seldom wore black—except to funerals. But no one I knew had died.

Puzzled, I looked around. There was nothing to see except a flight of wide marble steps leading to a massive pavilion. As I ascended, the air seemed to be thickening. The sun was gone and I seemed enmeshed in a heavy gray fog. On the pavilion the fog changed to a dismal blue mist swirling around tall white Corinthian columns that stretched from the marble floor into the mist above. Between the columns were small clusters of people talking in muted tones.

For a long moment, I merely stood at the top of the stairs. Then with some surprise, I realized I knew these people. All were relatives or friends on my father's side of the family. Recognizing my cousin I touched her arm and asked, "Bette, what is this place? What are we waiting for?"

When she did not reply I asked again, but Bette didn't seem to know I was there. I moved from one group to another, always asking the same question but receiving no response. It came to me that no one could see me!

I began to wonder if I was dead and this was my entry into another world. But no, I felt very much alive. I knew I was waiting for something or someone. I crossed the pavilion and stood beside one of the tall columns. The waiting seemed endless as I watched for a break in the thick blue mist. Then, a streak of silver light suddenly pierced the fog and opened a sparkling pathway through the sky.

Surprisingly I felt no fear. I knew I had to keep my eyes focused on the pathway. From a very great distance a solitary figure was approaching. As the figure came closer I saw it was a woman. Although I could not see her features because of the veil she wore, somehow I recognized my aunt, Bernice Silber. As she came nearer, the familiar scent she always wore reached my nostrils.

At last we stood facing each other. I moved to kiss her cheek through the heavy veil and she clung to me in a manner quite different from her usual reserve. She said, "Hi, honey, how are you?" Her voice was wistful. She continued to cling to me as if she might never see me again.

I answered, "I'm fine, Aunt Bee. How are you?"

Then she stood back from me and replied softly, "I just died, Jeaneane."

The dream ended. I awoke with a start. My bedroom was normal and peaceful, but I was filled with a horrendous fear. Of course I knew Aunt Bee had cancer and had been ill for a long time. But she lay in Deaconess Hospital in St. Louis, Missouri, and we had no reason to think her death was imminent.

Like a child afraid of the dark, I pulled the sheets over my head, my whole body quivering and perspiring. More than the dream, something else was frightening me—the heavy perfume lingering in my nostrils. I tried to tell myself I was an adult and shouldn't behave this way. And above all, my aunt was not dead! Why should I be afraid? Still, I couldn't move until the ring of the telephone forced me back to reality.

Craving the contact of a human voice I bounded from bed and grasped the phone. The voice was my mother's calling from St. Louis. She said, "Jeaneane, your Aunt Bee died during the night."

—*Jeaneane M. Rigioni, St. Charles, Mo.*

My Dream Won Against the Odds

The thought of turning psychic experiences to profit inevitably occurs to all of us. After all, it is only man's nature to conjecture, "Ah! If I could have the clairvoyance to know next year's Derby winner!"

Occasionally you hear that someone has dreamed of a winner and somewhat less occasionally you hear that his "dream horse" actually won. So you think to yourself, "How lucky! But that couldn't happen to me. I never dream of horses."

Well, I did. Just once.

About seven years ago, living in South Africa, I became interested in psychic matters and I felt increasing powers of intuition. I had been married for a couple of years to a young South African whose family owned and trained racehorses. Naturally, the sporting world absorbed my husband and we regularly attended the races. Thus I came to know at least the names of many South African racehorses, but there my interest and knowledge ended. To tell the truth, the whole subject often bored me. Needless to say, my attempts at betting usually proved disastrous!

Then one night I awakened abruptly from a vivid dream hearing the sound of a man's deep voice shouting a name: "Turfmaster!" I became wide-awake, knowing I had been dreaming about a race and had seen horses racing toward the finish line. I also knew that in my dream Turfmaster was the winning horse.

My husband, not yet asleep, asked what had startled me. I him about my dream and at only the head of the winner had appeared to me. The other horses were shadowy. Clearest of all was the impression of sound. The loudness of a man's strong voice shouting the name had awakened me.

My husband reminded me that a horse named "Turfmaster" actually existed.

The dream had left me with impression that the horse had some connection with the Cape Province, so I asked my husband to find out if it might be entered in a race there.

I never had dreamed about horse racing before. Could it be a prediction? My husband suddenly became very interested. He jumped out of bed, found a newspaper, and turned eagerly to a list of runners in the racing column. To our astonishment we found Turfmaster was due to run at our local course in Pietermaritzburg three days hence! We also were intrigued to learn that the horse had been bred in the Cape Province. However, my excitement soon subsided when my husband dryly remarked that the horse hadn't won a race in two years and in fact was regarded as "a bit of an old donkey!"

"If he wins, it will pay a fortune," he said.

I realized he meant the horse hadn't the remotest chance of winning. Nevertheless, the following Saturday found us at Scottsville Racecourse in Pietermaritzburg. I was curious to see Turfmaster, but alas, the sleepy white horse despondently walking the parade ring destroyed my confidence in the dream. The remarks of friends and relatives were scathing, for Turfmaster was considered one of the farthest-out outsiders in the race. At the last minute, however, my husband placed ten bob ($1.50) on the horse, just to please me.

The starter's gate went up. I waited tensely for the commentator to give the horses' positions.

Of course, Turfmaster trailed the field. Knowing the odds, I turned away. I spoke to my brother-in-law who was standing on a seat closely following the horses. Seeing my despondent expression, he teased me a little about my dream. As I climbed up beside him, he suddenly grabbed my arm and began to shout "Turfmaster! Turf-master!" at the very top of his voice.

I couldn't see a thing in the denseness of the excited crowd and I thought he was teasing me—a predilection of his—so I vigorously shook him and told him to stop it. The horse couldn't possibly have made up that much ground!

But Turfmaster had! He was streaking through to a photo finish! Again, my companion yelled the horse's name in jubilation and suddenly I recognized the sound of his powerful voice as the one that had sounded so deaf-ening in my dream.

I ran to my husband, whom I found confidently wait-ing at the winner's box for the jockey to return! For the small bet we had placed we took back £18 ($50)!

Of course, now that my dream had become real-ity, everyone wanted to know why I hadn't placed more money on the horse.

"That sort of dream," they assured me, "comes only once in a lifetime!"

I guess that must be true. Many of my dreams since have accurately predicted events, but no more friendly tipsters inspire my nocturnal life.

If you should have such an experience, don't be shy of telling someone about it immediately, and always make a note of the time and date. If you dream of lucky winners, however, I shouldn't tell too many people—for obvious reasons!

—*Kit Read*

Dream Pictures Guide Me

Dreams always have played an important role in my life. Even when I was young, only three or four years old and growing up in Adams, Massachusetts, dreams would warn me in advance that one of my frequent bouts with tuberculosis was approaching.

The dream never changed. In it I would see a tiny little man inhaling until his body had swelled so enormously that it nearly filled the room and left me crowded in a corner gasping for breath.

When I awoke, I knew I would be ill in a few days and I would warn Mother. Then just before the breaking of the fever I would dream I was in a deep cave where a beautiful waterfall dashed cooling spray high into the air.

These dreams continued until after the birth of my first child.

When I married in 1906, I moved with my husband Albert Wooden to Waterbury, Connecticut. Our lives there were peaceful enough until the tragic death in 1912 of our second child, Dorothy, from meningitis. Shortly before her death, I had a dream that I was walking on a narrow footpath through a dismal swamp, a child holding fast to each hand. Suddenly the little one slipped off the path and try as I would, I could not keep her from sinking downward into the deep mud. She was sucked into that awful swamp right before my eyes.

Crying hysterically, I roused my husband. I told him Dorothy was going to die. Angered, he pointed out that she was perfectly well. But three weeks later, she was dead.

We buried her on Christmas Day. This experience, my first with death, affected me so strongly that when Dorothy was buried I was in shock. I couldn't even remember the location of her grave. Later, when I made plans to visit the cemetery, I would become hysterical and finally a doctor forbade me to go near her grave.

Then one night the next September, I dreamed that I walked to the cemetery and found my way directly to her grave as if I had been going there regularly. I saw something very strange happening: the grave was opening slowly, folding back from the center like the leaves of a book.

From it my child emerged, a sad expression on her face. When I asked her the reason for her sadness, she answered that my constant grieving was holding her to earth when she should be traveling on to higher spheres. She begged me to grieve no longer but to be happy—that as soon as I released her, she would be able to experience the joy found only in the spirit realm.

The next morning I rose and left for the cemetery knowing exactly what path to take to get there.

I found it without trouble. I went often after that— not to mourn but to receive renewal and peace.

My daughter appeared to me only once after that. Late in 1919, I had fallen seriously ill with a new TB attack. Sick as I was with fever, I knew I was not expected to recover.

As I lay there suffering helplessly, I began to dream. I was on the third floor of a large apartment house, which was on fire. Firemen were carrying out one after another of the occupants and finally word went around that all had been evacuated. But I had been completely overlooked! As flames crept closer and closer I could feel my whole body burning from the heat. Just when I had given up hope I heard a voice calling, "Mother! Come!"

There just outside the window was my little daughter—now not so little—hovering in the air on two huge wings.

"Crawl, Mother, crawl," she said. Somehow I managed to get to the window out onto those wonderful strong wings. When at last I slipped my arms around her neck she flew me down to a wide stretch of cool green lawn and then she was gone.

In the morning, I had recovered from my illness. Everyone was astonished except me.

The severity of my illness convinced my brother-in-law, Dr. Charles Bates, that I should move to California's more healthful climate. In 1920 we went to Los Angeles where I had to go to work at the Broadway Department Store to help make ends meet. Some nights I crawled into bed too exhausted to eat. Whenever things seemed especially hard, when it looked as if I couldn't go on for even one more day, I would have a recurring dream. It never varied.

I would see myself swimming in a deep pool, clear as crystal and just warm enough for comfort. (All my life

I had longed to swim but had been forbidden to learn because of my weak lungs.) Flowers more beautiful than any I have ever seen bloomed along the edges of the pool. Their scent was as heady as wine, and in my dream I swam from one clump to another, inhaling deeply.

The light was from neither the sun nor the moon, but it was a soft glow, which changed from one lovely shade to another illuminating the entire scene and contributing to the sense of complete and perfect peace.

After bathing, I stepped onto a path leading across green lawns dotted with flowering plants toward a mansion that I seemed never to reach. I always awakened just as I was about to arrive there. Somehow I knew that if I ever did arrive I would have left the earth plane for good.

In the morning, I would feel sufficiently renewed to carry on for the next few weeks. Then inevitably the exhaustion would return to be followed again by the dream and the renewal.

Another remarkable dream I had during this period was one in which I was being sent on an important mission which required me to cross a sort of inland sea. As I approached the shore, a terrible storm arose. Lightning flashed, thunder pealed, and mountain-high waves broke into thousands of hissing snakes' heads instead of foam. With no time for wonder or fear, I knew I must think of nothing but my mission. So I plunged into the water and reached the other shore unharmed.

My mission (whatever it was) accomplished, I would prepare to return. The storm was even worse now and

I prayed for help in crossing that wild water. Almost at once I saw approaching me a bridge of woven straw not over two feet wide and with sides only a few inches high. But since this bridge, surely the frailest ever laid across a stormy sea, was apparently the answer to my prayer, I stepped out on it after expressing thanks to the sender.

Miraculously, the bridge held my weight. The water under it was perfectly calm while on either side the storm raged unabated. I felt quite safe, however, even when, as I was about halfway across, two rattlesnakes appeared directly before me with their heads lifted, ready to strike. In my dream, I knew God would not bring me this far only to destroy me so I stepped over them, His name on my lips.

In a flash I was transported to the shore and the storm cleared as if by magic. The sun shone, birds sang, and I was overjoyed for I had proven that faith would carry me through whatever trouble might assail me.

And so it has continued throughout my long life. The dreams I have recounted here show the protection and guidance that has been given me over the years. From where do they come—except another plane of existence where a benign God watches over His children?

—*Beth Dene Aldrich*

4

Near-Death and Out-of-Body Experiences

The human soul is a tricky subject of nearly infinite debate and possibility. The theory that we are made from the stuff of stars lends credence to the idea that once we pass from our mortal forms, we become a part of the cosmos itself. Who's to say that the freedom of mobility is only limited to what we can physically experience in our bipedal bodies? Since the ancient Egyptians to modern Christianity, the out-of-body or near-death experience has been a key principle of the faith in an infinite life beyond our limitations here on Earth. People around the world and throughout time thought to have died have reported the experience of seeing the bright aura of a calming presence as they float away to voices of dead family members. To some, a hand is seen beckoning to them from out of time as they lay dying in their beds. And while many skeptics have attempted to debunk these occurrences as nothing more than the hallucinations caused by brains deprived of oxygen, I believe that there something more—beyond what our limited knowledge can explain about our souls.

The following tales of people who have been to the threshold of death and seen the light of the impending afterlife represent a very special group—those who have traveled to the very brink of the abyss, only to return to the corporeal selves to tell the tale. Perhaps it is fate that these fortunate souls have shared their vivid stories so that we may take in heart in knowing that beyond this life is something wonderful.

Across the Miles

Since the night my only child, David, first was placed in my arms 37 years ago there has been an unusually strong bond between us. David was born and raised in my parent's home in Onley, Virginia.

Widowed when my son was a small child, I never was able to spend enough time with him because I had to work. Later I had to leave him in my parent's care when I went to work in Washington, D.C.

David finished school during World War II, promptly enlisted in the Air Corp, and was sent abroad. On his return from Europe, he matriculated at the University of California. Later he returned to Washington, D.C., where I was employed, and we were happily reunited once more.

Several years ago, David left to take a job in Honolulu, Hawaii. We were again separated physically, but the warm flame of love between us continued to burn brightly.

In November 1964, I retired on disability and returned to Onley, Virginia, a small town on a tiny peninsula, where I had spent much of my girlhood. On January 14, 1965, my phone rang. It was a radiogram stating my son was critically ill in a Honolulu hospital from an accidental gunshot wound in the head. Would I give permission for surgery?

Despite the mental fog that engulfed me I managed to dictate a message of consent. I tried to call Honolulu but couldn't get through because of bad weather conditions. Onley was covered with eight inches of snow, snow was still falling, and I was alone.

I am a Catholic, so I started calling priests to say masses and fellow Catholics to pray. After a few hours I was able to get a call through to a cousin, who is a Washington, D.C., lawyer. He promised to call me as soon as he could talk with the Honolulu hospital.

The hours dragged. I prayed. I walked. One thing stands out vividly in my memory from all those hours. As I prayed, I would unconsciously finish each prayer by saying out loud to my son, "Keep fighting, Son. Fight."

Finally my cousin called and said David had survived the operation but that was all the doctors could say. They explained if my son lived there might be brain damage or paralysis from his head injury.

Since I was unable to fly to Honolulu, I could only wait for more news. At long last, phone calls and letters started coming in. I was informed that David was mentally alert but paralyzed on the left side. He continued to improve and late in May was fitted with a leg brace, a cane, and a special sling for his left arm. Then he was moved to Long Beach, California, for therapy.

I wrote to David again, giving him my phone number and asking him to call collect when he was able. Somehow, I felt it would be "my" call if I could pay for it. On July 6, he called me and seemed to be bubbling with cheerfulness. He told me the doctors called his recovery a miracle.

But his next words sent shivers down my spine. He said, "Mom, why did you leave Honolulu before I was well enough to talk to you."

"Son," I replied, "I wasn't there."

"But Mom," David insisted, "When I wanted to slip back into unconsciousness I heard your voice. I certainly know my own mother's voice. You said, 'Keep fighting, Son. Fight.'"

A miracle, yes, but I call it God's answer to prayer.

By what invisible power was my voice transmitted to my son—from the mainland United States to Honolulu, Hawaii—to call him back from death?

—*Louise Savage Mapp, Onley, Va.*

The Beckoning Light

John William Dunne's *An Experiment with Time* has prompted me to reveal the greatest emotional experience I've ever had, an experience in astral projection that happened, in Dunne's words, "one and all, to myself."

One night in 1949, I lay in bed on the verge of sleep. All was quiet and I experienced a sense of complete relaxation and peace. Just before losing consciousness, I began to feel a tingling in my toes, which gathered momentum as it surged through my body. As it reached the top of my head, I felt a violent pull upward, not unlike the sensation I always feel before the climax to Wagner's opera *Tristan and Isolde*.

Suddenly, like the bursting of a taut elastic band, I was released. I was floating, a free agent capable of traveling with indescribable speed. I looked down and saw my body lying open-eyed on the bed, but I couldn't bother with what I had left behind on the bed.

I sped into space, turned somersaults in the air and marveled at how close I was to the stars. Never before have I seen such radiant colors.

Without willing where I was going, I had passed through the closed door of my bedroom and just as suddenly rushed out through the walls.

Again I was pulled far up into the heavens. In the distance I saw a white light, which became more and more dazzling as I approached. The whiteness was so blinding it compared to nothing I ever had seen.

Afraid to face that light although it beckoned me to come, I turned back. I felt then as though I was in a vacuum. Gone was the speed. All was deathly quiet, yet I heard a far off echo "speaking unspeakable words," as St. Paul said.

The most beautiful voice I've ever heard said, "Love the Lord thy God first." The last word was forceful and final.

Then I was back in bed, tingling from head to toe. I often have asked myself what would have happened had I walked into that light. I suppose I just wasn't a big enough person to accept that beckoning. I hope I'll be given the chance again.

—*Genevieve McGarigle, San Diego, Calif.*

Together Again

A serious catastrophe caused me the loss of my girlfriend, Myrtle Thayer, on March 17, 1959. I did not see her again for many years. Today, through the use of ESP, we are back together.

The morning after her disappearance I went about doing things as usual, but in a robotized consciousness. It seemed I was being guided by an irresistible, gentle voice, sometimes audible and clear, sometimes merely a murmur. I would pick up a paper, a book, or my Bible and open it at random. When I glanced at a page, certain words or phrases became three-dimensional.

Sometimes I would sit, staring at nothing, and a misty form would appear. It always took the form of a woman in a white dress, about five-foot-seven, the exact shape of my girlfriend Myrtle. At first the figure was headless, stood motionless for a few seconds, then disappeared.

After several appearances, I spoke to the misty form in a pleasant voice: "Hello, friend."

This time it stayed a little longer. As we became better acquainted it began to extend its visits. I would say, "Hello, dear," always speaking in a soothing voice, "You are a woman, aren't you?" The head would nod slowly. It never spoke audibly, only by signs or movements.

Sometimes the form would point to a certain book in my bookcase. I would take out the book indicated, open it, and find a phrase that answered my question or directed me to do something.

On one of these appearances, I was directed to open a small magazine relating stories on extrasensory perception. I understood from this that I could talk with my protoplastic friend without verbal conversation.

I thought, "Do you know where my sweetheart is?"

Immediately the form answered, "Yes, I am she. I was in a car accident the evening I left you. I'm in a hospital, alive but unconscious. Stay where you are, I'll find you. Wait! I can't remember clearly; my body must be healed again. It will take awhile; I don't know how long, for my neck is broken."

I asked my transparent friend, "Is there any way I can help you? I have already contacted the missing persons bureau with no results."

The misty white form replied, "Not just now! I will come to you again when I'm feeling better."

I waited another week, a month, a year, two years. My misty maiden came no more. I tried to forget her, but I remained single.

On the morning of July 3, 1964, as I sat in a chair quietly relaxing, my long lost, misty friend suddenly reappeared.

I greeted her with surprise. "Hello! I thought something awful had happened to you."

I received her reply through thought transference: "No, nothing bad has happened. It will take only a short while now, for my body is almost healed. If you will go to the local laundromat on August 2nd, there will be a bigger surprise for you."

On the designated day I gathered up my soiled laundry and went to the laundromat. I selected a machine and started to put my clothes into it.

Suddenly I heard a familiar voice "Well look who's here!"

I turned in amazement to see my sweetheart, whom I hadn't seen in the physical body for so many years.

Lost in astonishment at this miraculous meeting, we stood speechless.

Finally, Myrtle explained her disappearance, "The day I left you there was a five-car collision caused by a loaded gravel truck that went out of control wrecking four cars. It tipped over on mine, demolishing it. The rescue squad had to pry the doors open to get me out. My neck was broken and my memory impaired. I've tried to remember your last name and address, but just couldn't somehow. I thought of going to the dance where we first met, hoping to find you there.

"Darling," she said, "thank God, here we are together after all these years."

—*Albert Keltner, Bloomington, Calif.*

Home for Christmas

Opening our gifts on Christmas Eve always was a festive family custom, but Christmas Eve, 1944, was rather somber. For the first time my brother Willy, who was in the Navy, wasn't with us. We had not heard from him for several weeks. We tried unsuccessfully to hide our worry from each other, but when my mother suggested we go to bed early we readily agreed.

I was just drifting off to sleep when I heard strange noises downstairs. I sat up in bed and peered into the darkness of the upstairs hall, listening intently to shuffling steps and heavy, labored breathing. The sounds seemed to come from somewhere near the foot of the stairs. A voice moaned, "Dear God, they can't hear me!"

With a sudden feeling of dread—not fright; I wasn't at all frightened—I recognized the voice as my brother's and knew he was there at the foot of the stairs. He seemed to be fighting for breath, and I heard him moan again as he started to climb the stairs. As he climbed, I became aware of other, incongruous sounds, as though he were wading in deep water. The wet splashing grew more distinct as he neared the top of the stairs. I heard water squish under his shoes when he stepped onto the landing.

It was too dark to see him, but I felt his presence! I knew he was standing just beyond the open door of my room; and I knew without seeing him that he was soaking wet. I could hear water dripping from his clothing onto the floor.

"They don't know I'm gone," he said with a hopelessness that jarred me out of my trance-like state. I tried to speak to him, to reassure him, but before I could say a word he was gone. I didn't hear or see him go. I just knew he was gone.

I must have yelled because the light in the hall went on and in a few minutes the family was gathered around my bed, trying to convince me it had been a bad dream. They didn't succeed. I was so sure Willy had been there that I got up and examined the carpet on the landing and stairs for wet spots. There weren't any. But even that couldn't convince me I had been dreaming.

My final words as my mother turned out the light and left the room were, "You can believe it was a dream if you want to, but I know he was here even if he wasn't here!"

Two weeks later we finally got a letter from my brother. He was in a hospital in England, recuperating from exposure and shock. On Christmas Eve, during a violent storm, he had been swept overboard from the deck of a sub-chaser, in enemy waters, and had been near exhaustion when finally located and rescued hours later.

When he came home on convalescent leave a month or so later, he described his ordeal in detail. At one point, while the ship was leaving him behind and disappearing into the storm, he had shouted after it, but the roar of the wind and water had drowned his voice and he had moaned, "Dear God, they can't hear me!"—the very words I heard him say! His greatest fear was that no one would discover he was missing until too late, hence his statement, "They don't know I'm gone," which I also heard and which he had said over and over to himself while in the water. He said that finding himself utterly alone in that stormy expanse of night and water was more terrifying than the thought of dying. When he realized he was starting to panic, he invoked a mental picture of Christmas Eve at home; the tree, the family singing carols, eating fruitcake, and drinking spiced apple cider. After a while the pictures became so real he felt as though he actually were at home.

And he was home. While his corporeal body treaded water in the Atlantic more than 3,000 miles away, some nonphysical part of his being stood on the landing outside my room, spoke audible words in a recognizable voice, and dripped nonmaterial water onto the carpet. Either that or we were in telepathic communication and I hallucinated the sounds.

Twenty years have passed, but at family get-togethers we refer to 1944 as "the year Willy came home for Christmas."

—E. J. Tamion, Santa Fe Springs, Calif.

Saved by an Invisible Hand

I live on a hilltop overlooking Los Angeles, California. Although there is a well-lighted paved street winding down the hill from my home, I often take a short-cut down what used to be a narrow path through the grounds of Southwest Museum, which covers the hillside below my property.

On a night in 1957, when these grounds were still heavily wooded, I was in a hurry to get to a lecture on time, so I ran down the mountain path through the trees. It was too dark to see the path, but I knew the way even in the dark. I had been down this path many times at night without a thought of danger, but on this night when I got about halfway down the hill, I suddenly stopped short. It was as if a hand were pressed against my shoulder. I wondered what was wrong and tried to peer through the dense foliage of the Chinese cherry trees that covered the hill.

I remembered previously seeing some empty liquor bottles strewn on the ground under the trees, so I thought there might be a drunken man lurking in the bushes. I even thought there might be a snake on the path, although both these possibilities seemed doubtful because I usually can sense the presence of a person or animal.

I never have been afraid of the dark and, because I could not sense any "living" danger, I tried to continue on down the hill. But I could not take one step forward. This was disturbing enough, but then I felt myself moving backwards up the hill, as if pushed by an unseen force. I kept arguing with myself all the way, mentally saying it was ridiculous to go all the way back up the hill and down the long way on the paved street when I was in a hurry. This long detour would make me quite late for the lecture. This never had happened before and I was annoyed. Nevertheless, I was forced to do it.

I wondered about it all through the lecture and on my way home. I did not even try to take the shortcut going home. I could hardly wait for morning so I could go down the hill and see if there was any logical reason for what happened.

As soon as it was light the next morning, I ran down the hill again to see if I could find an answer. When I came to the place in the path where the invisible hand had stopped me the night before I again stopped short— with a gasp and cold chills up and down my spine. I was standing on the brink of a cliff that had not been there a few days before. Bulldozers were ranged down below; many trees had been uprooted, and half the hill had been cut away. They were building a new road where only a path had been before.

Without the forceful restraint, I would have plunged over the cliff.

—*Eleanor McBean, Los Angeles, Calif.*

Man in a Rowboat

Mildred Johnson and I visited Rye Beach, New York, on July 4, 1938. An excellent swimmer, Mildred decided to swim out to the breakwater a mile distant. Although only a mediocre swimmer, I bravely followed. Since the breakwater, a natural rock formation, was connected to the other end of the curved beach, I knew we would not have to swim back.

Fortunately, I was able to rest twice during the long swim, once on a float and again at the anchor of a moored yacht. While I was resting the second time, Mildred already had reached the breakwater and was sunning herself.

After this breather I continued my swim, but halfway to the breakwater I suffered a cramp and went under, gulping water. Terrified, I gulped more water and went under a second time. As I surfaced I prayed, "Oh, God, don't let me die."

A second later, I heard the voice of a fair-haired, blue-eyed young man. He was in a rowboat. "Hang on," he said. "I'll pull you over."

Gratefully I grasped the stern of the boat. We reached the breakwater, and with a word of thanks, I scrambled up the rocks. "It's time you got here," Mildred said.

"No thanks to you," I replied. "If that man had not rescued me, I would have drowned."

"What man?" she asked.

I scanned the horizon to point to my rescuer. In that short time he could not have traveled more than 100 feet, but the waters around us were empty. He had disappeared.

Years later, my father and I found a photograph album among the possessions of a recently deceased aunt. Opening the album, I studied the pictures of our relatives, living and dead. Abruptly I stopped before the smiling portrait of my father's brother, Herman Scommoday, who had died before I was born. This blue-eyed, blond young man had been my rescuer at Rye Beach.

—*Marlene Brenner, Bogota, N.J.*

"Get Out"

Mrs. Henrietta W., who lived on a 40-acre farm near Oakville, Iowa, became uneasy early in July 1965, feeling that her house was haunted. It frightened her. She could hardly bear to go into it.

On July 17, 1965, she was awakened by a loud clashing sound from another room. She went to look but everything seemed to be in order. Uneasily, she went back to bed. Then she heard footsteps outside her bedroom. Recognizing them, she got up and opened her door. Her dead husband stood there.

He said, "Get the h--- out of this house." Then he disappeared.

Frightened, not knowing what to do, she went back to bed just before a heavy bolt of lightning struck the house near her bed. She only came back to consciousness when her nightclothes caught fire and she managed to stumble out of the house just in time.

Her son, who heard the bolt, but did not know his mother was in the house until she came out, took her to a hospital in her bare feet and with a sheet around her. Fortunately her house and furniture were insured, the house for $7,000 and her furniture for $5,000. She still is slightly deaf from the lightning bolt, but her hearing is improving.

—*Nelle Van D. Smith, Newton, Iowa*

Unexpected Astral Call

In 1934 I entered the Booth Memorial Hospital in New York City for a major operation. The rather new anesthetic given me, due to my unusual reaction, quickly freed my soul from my physical body.

I saw that a radiantly beautiful angel stood guard at my head and another at my feet. I was freed from all pain and feelings of limitation, but still I was unable to tell those doctors and nurses who hovered anxiously about me, thinking I was "dead" because my breathing, heart, and pulse had stopped, that I was merely out of the body, safe and conscious.

So I left them and proceeded to make various journeys, guided by spiritual beings. Some of these journeys seemed to be to realms of great peace, love, and wisdom.

Then I went across the continent to visit my special friends, Charles and Pearl Sindelar, in Los Angeles, California. Charles Sindelar was the renowned artist who painted the famous Christ Head from a "so-called vision." It was very early morning in California, as it was only 8:00 a.m. in New York, but they both awoke, saw me and exclaimed, "It's Enid! I wonder what's the matter."

Later that same morning they telephoned my father, Melvin Severy, who also lived in Los Angeles. But he knew nothing of my operation as I had wished not to worry him. He promised to write to me immediately.

From his letter, I was able to verify the fact that I had appeared to my friends in California at exactly the time of my passing out of my body in New York City, allowing, of course, for the difference in time between the two sections of the country, and a slight variation in clocks.

This was the last time I ever "saw" my friends, Pearl and Charles, so for many reasons my astral call had significance.

Meanwhile, in the operating room in Booth Memorial Hospital the doctors were so sure I had died that they left me, to attend to other patients. When I did ultimately return to my body, I was wheeled back to my room without having the operation I had gone up for. This operation was then successfully performed a day or two later.

—*Enid S. Smith, Mesa, Ariz.*

Among the Dead

In July 1965, I spent two weeks in the psychiatric ward of a hospital in North Vancouver, British Columbia. A hard life and a difficult menopause had led to my complete nervous breakdown.

Electric shock treatments and medication can cause one to forget temporarily those experiences that caused the collapse and emotional imbalance. Afterward the memory returns completely, but the return is gradual, giving the individual opportunity for emotional rest and the nerves time to regain strength. Psychological help is given also over long period of time to help the rehabilitation. It was in this manner that I received help.

Before each shock treatment, I was given a hypodermic and by the time I was wheeled into the treatment room, I was only dimly conscious of a white masked figure prodding the inner side of my arm with a needle.

Then came a terrible roaring inside my head. The roaring increased; then, suddenly, my skull seemed to explode into a thousand tiny pieces.

On one occasion when I became fully conscious again, it was dark—the deepest, softest darkness I have ever known. There was complete silence and no movement of any kind. I wondered where I was, but it was so peaceful, so wonderful I decided to rest awhile.

Just when I became aware that I was without my body I am not sure, but it was a shock. "Dear Lord, I'm dead," I thought. "I must be dead if I haven't a body."

Yet a great tide of happiness flooded over me. I was not afraid. I could think; I could feel; I was completely normal—only I didn't have a body!

There are no words in the human vocabulary to describe the rest, the peace, the exquisite joy I experienced. I became conscious of "knowing." I still was quite alone, but Someone was communicating with me, instructing me in the understanding of creation. I can remember only some of the things I learned.

Then all became blank.

When I was conscious again my family was standing around my hospital bed. I felt dazed and stupid. My tongue was chewed and bleeding. I was stiff and sore. I managed to ask my husband the time.

"It's evening, dear. You have slept all day. How do you feel?" he answered. I noticed he looked strained and pale.

I didn't tell anyone at the hospital of my experience. I confided it only to my family. But it remained a bright, vivid oasis in my memory. In some strange way it helped me recover from the complete nervous breakdown much more rapidly than expected. At the end of two weeks, I was back home with my loved ones.

I visited my psychiatrist every two weeks for some time and on one such visit, about three months after my hospital stay, I asked him if he had been present during my three shock treatments. He assured me he had.

"Something went wrong during one of them," I said. "I will tell you what happened on the inside if you will tell me what happened outside."

He agreed and then wrote down my case records the same story told here.

When I had finished he fulfilled his side of the agreement.

"After you were anesthetized, the electrodes were applied to your temples," he said. "You went into a violent convulsion. You threshed about so wildly with your limbs and body, it was all we could do to hold you. Then everything stopped. You were dead for several minutes before we were able to revive you."

—*Laurette B. King, North Vancouver, British Columbia, Canada*

I Tried to Bribe a Ghost

The night of June 19,1943, was one I'll never forget. Its events surpassed all understanding. I wrestled with a ghost and when he subdued me, I tried to bribe him.

The evening began when my girl friend Elsie Hulk asked me to go to a dance with her. Although my husband-to-be, Matt Murphy, was a soldier and on duty that night, I decided to go anyway. For that matter, Elsie was supposed to have worked that night but with the irresponsibility of the young we jumped into her coupe and took off for the dance, arriving about nine o'clock.

Elsie's pink blouse had led me to pick a bunch of rose-buds from my garden to pin in her hair. They matched her blouse exactly and she looked very pretty.

The place was Renton, Washington, a city that was bursting its seams in 1943. Boeing Aircraft operated at peak capacity and radar units encircled the town. Defense workers and soldiers poured into the city every weekend and on this Saturday night all of them seemed to be in the dance hall.

Having worked as a USO hostess, Elsie knew many of the soldiers. She started dancing the moment we arrived and never sat down again. However, I had become engaged the week before and felt guilty being there at all while my soldier was on duty. I sat until 11 o'clock, alter-nately declining invitations to dance and admiring my engagement ring.

Suddenly, I was seized from behind by a pair of very strong hands. My arms were snapped so violently to my sides that the breath was forced from my lungs. My purse flew from my hands to the floor.

I jerked around to free myself from what I thought was a very poor joke, but although my arms were held in a vise-like grip, I saw that no one stood anywhere near me. Some force pushed me to my feet and at the same time a man's voice said, "Go home!"

Even then, I realized I had not actually heard the voice. It seemed to project itself into my mind like a burst of light.

My back was held rigidly against a man's chest. Again the words exploded in my mind: "Go home. Go home!"

Now anger took over and I twisted and turned trying to get loose. I particularly wanted to retrieve my purse. I screamed to Elsie, but the noise of the music and dancers drowned my voice. I hoped a couple sitting nearby would help me, but the woman simply turned to the man and shrugged.

My feet dragged as I was carried toward and out the door. Strange as it sounds I did not feel frightened. Whatever was pushing me only made me angry. I began to plead to be allowed to get my purse.

"It has my ration book in it! Think of all the trouble I'll have if I lose it."

"No!" exploded the voice. "You must go home now!"

Well, home was a mile-long walk along a four-lane highway. Traffic was fairly heavy and three cars stopped—then sped away without anyone speaking a word. I have no idea what they thought about a young lady furiously running along a highway.

Now gasping for breath, I tried once again to explain about my purse. I promised I would leave the dance hall as soon as I got it back. My invisible companion didn't even bother to answer.

Then I was home and in record time too. My companion pushed me against the front door and when I turned the knob I was flung into the hall.

"Stay here!" This time I heard the voice, and for the first time I was frightened by its dictatorial tone, as if to say if I disobeyed I would be severely punished.

I slammed the door, quickly pushed back the curtain, and flicked on the porch light. There was absolutely no one in sight on the porch, in the front yard, or in the street.

I went into the kitchen and sat down at the table, thinking over this strange experience. It took me an hour to calm down and then I went to bed. But of course I couldn't sleep. I tossed and turned until dawn and finally got up and went down to the kitchen again. I felt a dull ache in my arms and shoulders, a reminder of the rough treatment of the night before.

I was drinking coffee when my neighbor Ted Siplia, along with a state patrolman came into the house. They simply walked through the door and stood in the hall. (In this quiet neighborhood where I had lived all my life, no one ever locked a door.)

"I'm here in the kitchen," I called out. "What's the matter?"

When he saw me, my neighbor almost fainted.

"You're dead!" he babbled. "You were killed last night. They identified you by your ration book...." He was almost crying.

Gradually regaining control of himself, Ted told me what had happened. Elsie and a soldier companion had left the dance to get something to eat. On the big highway they had hit a Greyhound bus head-on. My purse, picked up from the dance hall floor by my friend, contained the only woman's identification recovered from the terrible wreck.

At the morgue I identified her—the pink roses were still in her hair. Her companion I didn't know.

My fiancé Matt said later that he had had an awful premonition about me that night. He hadn't known I went to the dance, but he kept seeing me crushed and bloody in his radarscope! The presentiment became so overwhelming that he got down on his knees right there by the instrument and prayed for help. A deeply religious person, he prayed long and fervently. He was frightened but he believed God would help me.

I can't pretend to explain what happened but whoever or whatever the force was—ghost or angel—I've thanked him a thousand times for being unbribable.

—*Joyce DeMerrelle, Seattle, Wash.*

A Crucial Reentry

In the spring of 1944, I turned 10 years old. I was a healthy youngster and never had had asthma until that spring. (Old-timers said the fruit pollen was so thick that year you could see it in the air.)

When a violent attack of bronchial asthma threatened to stop my breathing entirely, my frantic parents thought I had pneumonia. Before the doctor could arrive, my chest became so congested that I passed out. My next conscious feeling was the realization that I suddenly had been released from the aching back and desperate gasping that accompany severe asthma. All at once I felt peacefully relaxed and free. Floating above everything in my bedroom, I could see my lifeless body. The vague thought that I was dead penetrated my consciousness. It didn't seem to bother me at all. I enjoyed this great feeling of freedom.

I remember not wanting to return to that tortured body but when the doctor arrived, he quickly injected a powerful dose of adrenalin into my lifeless form. I began to feel an irresistible force pulling me back into my flesh.

The excruciating pain I experienced on reentering my body is indescribable. Had I been free to choose, I think I never would have returned from the free spiritual state I had known for so short a time.

—*R. Frederick Taylor, Las Vegas, Nev.*

Haunted Places

There are places in this world that defy explanation. Homes, business, castles, and even caves that seemingly contain a paranormal presence have been found all over the world. Some of these mysterious places are more easily identified than others. Spaces in which gruesome murders were committed often leave a spiritual stain haunting its cursed confines. Sometimes the combined accumulation of many deaths over the years can account for the presence of spirits that refuse to move beyond the lives they once knew; forever forced to share their former residence with the current occupants. And we are hard pressed to find someone who does not know of a place that seems to have an energy all its own.

One of our greatest fears is being unfortunate enough to choose a residence in the same vicinity as ghostly haunting. In every town across the world, the idea of the haunted place or house has been recognized since long before any type of recorded history. The haunted caves and forests of old have given way to homes and roads that contain the spectral energy of the ghosts who claim these places.

And while haunted houses remain the spooky mainstay of Halloween gatherings and county fairs, the real haunted houses that seem to lurk in every town will always inspire more fear than any wobbly mirrors. These places are as real as the weary people who speak of them, but only in whispers with crawling goose-pimpled skin. The dark and foreboding house with the reputation of strange occurrences. Those places that seem to have a living presence despite its artificial nature will always be the stuff of childhood dares, and now *FATE* dares you to turn the page and read the collected offerings of the spookiest of haunted places.

"That Thing"

In 1928 I was living with my sister, Marie, and her husband, Alford Dodson. They had a four-year-old daughter, Dorothy, and I had a boy of the same age, named Allen. My husband was working at a government hospital and had to live in the men's barracks, as they didn't have a place for families.

My brother-in-law worked as a carpenter for a big mining company that owned the houses their employees lived in. They furnished rented homes according to the size of the families. We had a one-bedroom house with a large sleeping porch, as this was during the Depression and we didn't have much money. Our house was badly in need of paint and repairs, so we decided to look for another one.

We found the very house we wanted, went to the rental office and told the man what we wanted to do. He told us we couldn't have that particular house. But when we asked why, he couldn't give us a good reason and finally told us to go ahead and move in—but not to come back in a few weeks wanting another house. We promised him we would be very happy in our new home.

He gave us the key and we lost no time in moving in. From the very first moment, I felt someone was breathing on the back of my neck. We had a big German police dog that went around with her hackles raised and a low growl deep in her throat.

Alford, working the swing shift, went to work at 2:30 p.m. and got home around midnight. Marie and I would put the children to bed in the bedroom and then sit in the living room and crochet or play cards until her husband came home. We had been raised in the country and weren't afraid of anything. But the children began to wake up crying and when we asked them what was wrong they told us, "That old man hurt us." Finally they refused to stay in the bedroom.

Next, the dog took to howling in the middle of the night, so we let her sleep in the kitchen. When we went in to see about her, she would be lying on the floor with her paws on her head and looking for all the world like she had been whipped. She began to lose weight and got real thin.

We would lock the kitchen door on the inside with a skeleton key and then give the key another half-turn so no one could push the key out. Nevertheless, every morning the door would be standing wide open. One morning there was a brand-new, shiny key in the door even though I had locked it with the old key the night before.

Finally I told Marie I was going to move my bed out into the sleeping porch even if I froze, and if that thing came out there, I was going to move. That night our youngest brother came to stay all night and we put him on the lounge in the front room. Toward morning I heard someone come out of the bathroom, go through the bedroom into the front room, and on into the kitchen. They had their shoes on and it sounded like a cane tapping the floor. I called to my brother thinking that he might be walking in his sleep. When he didn't answer, I got up and went into his room but he was in bed, fast asleep. I went back to bed and to sleep.

About daylight next morning when I woke up, turned over, and started to reach for the alarm clock, this thing was bending over me, with its face not more than six inches from my face. I screamed, and it floated toward the outside door. It went right through a table and the closed door.

It was dressed in black with a sort of hood over its head. Where its face should have been there wasn't anything. It's been almost 35 years ago and I still freeze up when I think about it.

When we went back to the rental office all the man said was, "I told you SO!"

My husband got another job in another town about 40 miles away and we took our dog with us. But she got worse until she died.

Several years later, we went back to this town and drove along the street where we had lived. The house was gone and I was told that it had been moved to a new location. My husband talked to the sheriff there and he said that before he took office and during prohibition a bootlegger had lived in the house and had been shot and killed in the bathroom.

—*Lucille Harbour, Anderson, Calif.*

I Saw the Ghost

I always have been convinced that the house in which I grew up was haunted—this despite the fact that it was a new house, built the summer I was 15. The old house it replaced was built by my grandfather and was one of the first ever built in Pocahontas County, Iowa. It had not been haunted. Our new farm home was three miles northwest of the small Iowa town of Rolfe, and not equipped with electric lighting.

For years, it was only the noises that frightened me. I was 21 before I ever saw a ghost. These noises were principally rapping and footsteps, usually tramping about in the attic over my room but sometimes in the upstairs hall. There was also the sound of boxes being dragged about on the attic floor. And very often there was a sharp rap on my ceiling, as of someone tapping hard on the attic floor with a cane. There were several old canes up there, leaning against the wall. They had belonged to my grandfather. But when I went up to the attic in daylight to investigate, nothing ever seemed out of place. I think the most eerie sound of all was an omnipresent click. On the nights when "they" were there this soft, faint click seemed to be everywhere in the room. It was an unearthly sound that I never have heard anywhere else.

It is impossible to describe my terror on these nights. I often lay bathed in the cold sweat of fear. When things got too bad, I would go to my parents' room and wake them. There never was a time when they could not hear the same things I heard. But the strange thing is that otherwise they seemed to sleep right through it all. Neither they nor my younger brothers and sisters seemed frightened. As my parents' religious beliefs forbade a belief in ghosts, they would at first say it was my nerves. Then admitting they heard it too, they would say there must be some natural explanation, although they never offered one.

The summer I was 21 and back home after a year of teaching school, both by mother and I saw it! On a peaceful summer night about 10 o'clock, I was lying wide-awake in my bed. The whole family had retired early, as is the custom of farm people. Hearing a slight sound at my door, I looked to see the door open. There stood a man with his hand on the doorknob. He was dressed in a sort of overall, a light gray garment, like a suit of long underwear. The light was too dim for me to distinguish his features, but it seemed to be the figure of a young man. I tried to think it must be my brother, who occupied the room next to mine. I called his name, but he did not answer. I am not sure now whether I screamed and he then turned away, or whether it was the other way around. At any rate, he moved from the door, out of my vision, and my mother, hearing my screams, came from her room in time to see the figure leaving my door.

As she told it, she thought she saw my brother, Noble, dressed in his dark Sunday suit, walk away from my room and into his own. She followed into my brother's room and even on into the clothes closet, where the figure just disappeared!

She was in a state of great confusion and coming back said, "Why, wasn't Noble here?" But although Noble was sound asleep in his bed and she actually had seen this figure, and seen it vanish, she never admitted she had seen a ghost! Years later, when we argued over this she said it might have been a hallucination, to which I replied that hallucinations can't open doors, and this one did!

There is a sequel to this, but no conclusion, as I never have learned of any reason why this house should have been haunted. No crime, no murder, or tragedy ever took place there. No one even died there.

Some years after, I had married and come home for a visit, bringing my baby. I was given the one downstairs bedroom. I think it was the second night of my visit when I was waked out of a sound sleep by the distinct sensation of being rapped on the top of the head with a ruler or small stick. It was not a dream; it was a definite physical sensation and it gave me a rude shock! The room was pitch-dark. I could see nothing, but I was so frightened that I dashed upstairs to call Mother. She came downstairs with me, carefully closing the bedroom door, and got into bed with me. But we were no sooner in bed than the door reopened. I heard the creaking of its hinges. Then something like a small dog bounded across the wood floor. I could hear its claws as they struck the floor, but it was too dark to see anything. Whatever it was must have been running blind, for it would go "trr-ump, trr-ump, trr-ump, wham!" first bumping into one wall and then into the opposite wall, hard. After a few minutes of this, it seemed to gallop into the closet and we heard it no more.

My mother exclaimed in surprise, "I didn't know we had any rats in here!"

I answered, "That was no rat."

As soon as it went into the closet, she got up and closed that door in order to trap the "rat." She said she would let the dog in there the first thing in the morning. This she did but, of course, the dog found nothing.

As the farm passed out of my father's hands some time later, I have no way of knowing whether subsequent occupants were troubled by these hauntings.

—*Bernice Knapp, Chicago, Ill.*

Haunted House at Far Rockaway

I was a child when my mother came into her inheritance. Because her brother, Kenneth Reid, was a minor, the entire estate had been handled by an administrator. Their parents' house at Far Rockaway, Long Island, had been leased, but the renters had moved out angrily, declaring the house was haunted.

Mother had laughed. But Uncle Kenneth had insisted, "It is haunted, I heard the chains hurled down the stairway myself!"

Mother said gently, "Grandmother paid $16,000 for it and it should be worth double that now, with the Long Island Railroad running. But the Clevelands' offer is $8,000. Do you want to take that—or shall we hold out for more? Perhaps a real estate man could get nearer a fair price."

"I tell you," shouted my young uncle, who had just come of age, "I want out! I don't care if someone will pay $100,000, I want out now. You go East and get whatever you can out of it."

Mother looked startled. "I? You are of age. You go!"

But a week later, in late May 1900, Mother and I took the train to New York. My father, Robert John Montgomery, being an inventor, spent every spare cent he earned as a certified public accountant as well as stray income from Mother's estate and we always were hard pressed for money. So Mother and I did not take a Pullman, but sat up during the long train trip.

In the early part of the trip, Mother and I enjoyed looking out of the train window, but I grew very sleepy. I put my head on Mother's lap and dozed and then I went heavily asleep. Each time I roused, Mother was sitting wide-awake, looking more worn and tired.

Even after we reached New York City it was a long, tiresome trip to the Long Island house. When we reached the village, Mother could hardly drag along but she said, with an effort, "We'll stop at the restaurant and get some dinner."

At that moment we passed a delicatessen and, looking at the boiled ham in the window, I suggested we get some ham and a loaf of bread and some butter. "Maybe some eclairs, too," I added hungrily.

So as we walked out to the end of the shaded street to the house, we carried our big bag of clothes and some paper bags from the delicatessen shop. I could hardly wait to look at everything—the wide verandah that circled the big house, the huge coach house at the rear, the wide staircase in the lovely front ball. I had heard about it so many times I almost felt I was coming home.

Mother was not so pleased. She wrinkled her nose at the unmowed lawn, which was more weeds than grass, at the dust over everything.

After we had eaten our picnic she started up the curving stairway.

"Aren't we going to explore?" I asked.

"Let's go upstairs and rest a bit. I'm very tired."

In the big corner bedroom on the second floor, I was surprised to notice there was no dust as there had been downstairs. There was a wide, green velvet sofa across one corner of the huge room and Mother stretched out on this saying softly, "Bring me the scarf."

I knew the scarf. When she took a nap in the afternoon she always tied one end on her wrist and the other end on mine, so that I could not wander away.

"I don't need to be tied," I told her.

But she motioned toward the travel bag and I got out the scarf. Once I was tied to her wrist, she fell into a heavy sleep. I hoped she would not sleep too long as I was anxious to look at the whole house. But I must have dozed because when I waked, the windows no longer showed blue ocean and the whole room was very dark. There was only one light spot, the empty corner behind that green velvet sofa.

There seemed to be no source for light, but the corner was brilliantly lit. In fact, it was so bright I raised my hand to shield my eyes. It was then I saw the little man.

"Hello," I said. "Who are you?"

He just stood there looking at me pleasantly. Then he glanced down at my sleeping mother. His eyelashes were golden, very thick, and very long; they looked like almost golden fans lying on cheeks. He stretched out one hand toward, as I first supposed, mother, but then I saw the cat, a beautiful seal point Siamese cat that looked exactly like the one father and mother and I had seen the preceding Sunday at what father called the Fat Cat Show in the Coliseum in Chicago. I loved cats and almost always had one, but mine were just common alley cats.

The cat was climbing the man's outstretched arm along his grey jacket sleeve. It was then that I noticed the suit was the same light grey color as his wide-brimmed hat. As the cat climbed, the man whispered to it so softly that I could not hear his words but when the cat began to lick his cheek, the man laughed delightedly and murmured, "Kissin' cat, eh? Kissin' cat!"

Now the cat crawled around his beneath the brim of the hat almost resembled a fur neckpiece. The man stretched out one finger and the cat began to snarl and bite and claw in mock ferocity. "Oooh, that cat's going to bite me," the man said happily.

The cat, stretching out a paw, clawed at his jacket until one small raveling came loose. The man said thinly, "Now, now. Not too hard Little Doll Baby. Not too hard!" He picked the raveling from the cat's claw and dropped it to the sofa.

The brilliant light in which they were standing was too much for my eyes, and I suppose I dozed off again for when I waked the room was light and I could see the ocean surf, with high whitecapped waves, dancing in the morning sunlight.

I heard a knocking at the door and called Mother.

She opened her eyes swiftly, looking at me questioningly.

"It's someone at the front door," I whispered.

"You don't need to whisper, darling. Here, I'll loosen your end of the scarf and you run down to see who's there."

I opened the huge front door we had bolted the evening before and saw a white-haired man. A white-capped housemaid, stood beside him.

"You must be little Laura's daughter?" he asked.

"Come in, sir. I am Laura's daughter. I'm Lily. Mother is upstairs."

He seemed to take this as an invitation because he motioned the housemaid, who was, carrying a huge brass tray, to go ahead, upstairs.

"Judge Ely!" exclaimed Mother when we all entered the huge second-floor room. "I'm so happy to see you again."

"And I you," he replied, just like in a storybook I thought. "Put the tray down, Selma, and you may go back. I thought you might like to have a bite of breakfast Laura. I noticed yesterday that you looked fagged out when you came in and so I did not disturb you. I noticed the Clevelands driving by, too. I hear they are dickering for the house."

"Yes," Mother told him. "She wrote me they would offer $8,000 spot cash."

"Eight-thousand! Why child, your mother paid me $16,000 and I took that price because I was in a tight spot and needed cash. It's worth every cent of $25,000 now."

"She made the low offer because the house is haunted," Mother said. "Oh, of course, I don't believe it, you know. But Kenny is now of legal age and the place is half his. He wants to sell and so I really have no choice.

"You know Mrs. Hetty Green wanted to come here with my mother and share expenses for the summer— she had a son and daughter, too, so it would have been even, so to speak. Mother said no, she wanted her home to herself but she did invite them to stay a week or so until they could get accommodations at the hotel. Well, one night was enough—Hetty insisted that Mother had drawn chains up and down the stairs and had yelled. Of course, we hadn't. But Kenny swears up and down that he, too, has heard the chains and the yells. He insists on selling—at any price we can get."

"Is a haunted house always bad?" I asked. "I mean are the haunts or whatever—are they always mean and bad? I mean," I hesitated, "I mean—there was a man here in the night…"

"Nonsense," said my mother.

"But there was!" I insisted "A little man in a wide grey hat and he had a cat—a Siamese cat, Mama."

"You had a dream, darling. I saw no man."

"There was a cat, you say?" asked judge Ely. "Tell about it, Lily. Do you know the cat's name?"

"The man had long thick golden eyelashes. And the cat's name . . . that cat licked his face and the man called him Kissin' cat . . . then later on the man called him Little Doll Baby when the cat clawed a raveling from the sleeve of the man's jacket."

"Oh, what a tangled web we weave when first we practice to deceive," Judge Ely said sadly. "I should have told your mother about the Poppenhausens, Laura. They were Quakers and very fine people. The young ones had been missionaries to Siam, but the weather was too much for the young Poppenhausen, and he contracted quick consumption. They came here to hunt for a house where he could get ocean air. The doctors thought it might be beneficial. Tone him up, you know. They both had just come into money. They saw this house as yet unfinished, fell in love with it, and bought it. Even though the house wasn't finished they moved in, sleeping in the dressing room at the side there—just as your mamma did, Laura. And they spent their days looking out over the bay and the ocean. For a week or two, he seemed to improve and then there was the collapse and he died, right here in this room! She took him back to Philadelphia to be buried with the family and then she came back. Would I let her pay rent for the time they had occupied the house and cancel the sale? I did."

"So the house wasn't actually new as Mamma thought?" my mother exclaimed.

"That was when I first began to 'deceive,' as the proverb goes. Your mamma was glad there were things to be completed," the judge continued. "I had no intention of lying to her, but she commented: I'd hate to live in a house where anyone had died. Right then and there I should have told her about the Poppenhausens. No one in the village ever told her because the young man had been so weary, they stayed right here in the house and never saw anyone much nor went any place. Those long, thick golden eyelashes were the mark of the man, you might say."

"But the chains on the stairs?" Mother asked.

Judge Ely sighed, "Ah, yes. The chains…are you listening, Laura?"

Mother held up her hand; she had picked a raveling from the green velvet sofa and they stared at it. Judge Ely took it and handed it to me, "Put this into your pocketbook, Lily—the only memento you'll probably ever have of a real 'live' ghost."

"The chains?" Mother prompted.

"Yes, the chains. I owned all this property along here, you know, some 52 acres. On this spot there was a stone shelter with no windows only a low doorway. The door opened onto a slimy path leading to the water's edge. It ended in a cave, which was completely hidden at high tide and not very accessible at low tide. The children around claimed pirates had built a hideout right here on the point. We tore the stone shelter down and went ahead."

"If Lily hadn't slept so much on the train coming here," Mother mused, "she would have been asleep as I was and would have missed the visit of the Siamese cat and the Quaker man."

Then she said more briskly, "Judge Ely, I'll require them to sign a complete release in the event of any ghosts they may see or hear, or think they see or hear."

And Mother did just that. Later in the morning down at the bank where we met the Clevelands, Mother dictated the release to Mrs. Cleveland who mumbled and fussed at this, but the price they were offering was so clearly too little that both Clevelands realized Mother would not sell without it. Indeed, Mother's usually soft pink lips were in a straight, hard line as she dictated.

"Now, you may both sign this release," Mother said at the end.

"'This is nonsense," blustered Dr. Cleveland. "Ghosts! Indeed! All silly superstition."

Mother smiled gently. "I'm glad to hear you say so. You understand I make no claims that there are or are not ghosts in the house. However, we now have this paper, which I shall ask the president of the bank and his cashier to witness and sign. You have both heard the statements, gentlemen. I don't wish to have to make a trip back here later on to substantiate any of this. I now live in Chicago and it is a long, long train trip. Also, I wish to take the cash home with me, not a bank check."

It was only about a month later that Mother received a letter from Mrs. Cleveland saying, "You will have to return our purchase money at once. You knew well enough that the house was haunted, and to sell the house haunted was a misrepresentation. Kindly send the money at once and we will let the matter die and not sue you."

Of course, returning the money was out of the question. My uncle had his half and Mother's half had been dropped into the invention costs.

However, even had she replied at once, it would have been too late. Judge Ely wrote Mother that Dr. Cleveland had "fallen" down the beautiful circular staircase and that when they picked him up there were bruises on his neck and body "as if he had been chain-whipped."

We never heard from Mrs. Cleveland again.

In my childhood, my grandparents' house at Far Rockaway had no street address as it was in only a very small suburb. It was the second house from Jamaica Bay.

I went back there in 1939 to find the area all built up, with houses on 75- and 100-foot lots, so it was difficult even to tell the exact spot where our house had stood. The street is now called Bayswater Road.

My grandmother, Emma, and grandfather, Dr. Kenneth Reid, are in the Maple Grove Cemetery far from Far Rockaway. Father died in 1947; my mother, Alexandra Reid Montgomery, in 1950. My uncle, Kenneth Reid, who had heard the chains in his early youth, died in May 1959.

—*Lilliace Mitchell*

... And the Frisky Phantom

La Chaumiére, a French restaurant in Fordingbridge, England, is capitalizing on its friendly phantom. Its advertisements in the Bournemouth Times include the line: "P.S.: Even the Ghost is friendly!"

Reporter Warren Davis didn't believe the advertisement and decided to investigate. Taking his lawyer along as an independent witness, Davis was convinced within 10 minutes that the ghost really exists and dining out in such company can be a real adventure.

The restaurant is owned by a Bournemouth couple, Mr. and Mrs. John Harden. For two years they have sought an explanation but so far can only conclude the ghost means no harm. It gives their 17th-century business establishment (also their home) a unique and profitable fillip.

The reporter found the ghost has quite a sense of humor, which he manifests by sprinkling green paint around the house. Two years ago when the Hardens bought La Chaumiére, it had been a private house and needed redecorating. They decided to paint their own quarters themselves. The woodwork had been green, but they decided to paint everything white. This is when the trouble began. After a day's work the white paint-soaked brushes were left in turpentine. In the morning, the brushes were covered with fresh green paint, the shade that originally had been used in the room. Some mornings the newly painted white surfaces were speckled with green and one morning a small fireplace bore the green paint trademark of the mischievous miscreant.

During the next year, the Hardens were troubled by strange sounds, footsteps, and voices murmuring indistinct words. The green paint episodes continued. In a bathroom only last summer, a door that had three coats of white paint began to ooze liquid green paint—enough so that drops fell onto the floor.

The paint spots give visual confirmation of the presence of another "inhabitant" in the house and the Hardens could put up with that. But Mr. Harden grew annoyed with the noises and dramatically settled this problem. He had read of a breed of dog called a Shih Tzu kept by Tibetan lamas to ward off evil spirits. He went to considerable trouble to secure a Shih Tzu puppy and named him "Babu." From the moment of his arrival, there have been no more supernatural noises but the fresh spots of paint continue to appear. In fact, now it might be quite a loss to La Chaumiére if they didn't.

—*Curtis Fuller*

Guest Appearance

On the 25th of August, 1965, I was engaged in research work at the Public Library in Lake Worth, Florida. It was a surprise to me to see Karl Kroeger, the cousin of an acquaintance of mine, in the library that day. Karl was an annual winter visitor, usually arriving from Minneapolis in November. He was way ahead of schedule this year.

The library was his favorite hangout in Lake Worth. Now glancing up from his book he saw me and waved, then continued reading. He was merely an acquaintance and since he didn't seem inclined to chat, I continued my own work.

After that, I saw him almost daily. He'd wave, then continue reading. One day I encountered his cousin Lena Hutchins on the street.

"I see your cousin every day at the library, " I said casually. "He came to Florida much earlier this year, didn't he?"

"My cousin!" exclaimed Lena. "You mean Karl?" I nodded.

"Why, he died more than a year ago," Lena said. "He must have a double." I knew I was not mistaken. Karl, a tall, slender man had a rugged Lincolnesque face topped with white bushy hair. Further, he waved his hand in a characteristic way—as some Latins do—with fingers beckoning toward himself, not outward.

The next time I saw Karl at the library, I phoned Lena. She came at once and I was waiting on the library steps. Triumphantly, I led her into the reading room. Karl wasn't there! I rushed her through the other rooms. He was in none of them. Where could he have gone? He and his table had been in sight all the time and the library has only one entrance. He couldn't have left without my seeing him.

"Your imagination is playing tricks with you," jibed Lena. "I think you need a rest. Maybe you've been working too hard through this frightfully hot summer!"

Why did Karl Kroeger appear to me? Did he come in spirit to a favorite spot? And was I the only one capable of seeing him?

—*Carol Veronica Bird, Lake Worth, Fla.*

A Bad Investment

About four years ago my father bought an old house on Stonewall Avenue in Richmond, Virginia. He planned to refurbish it and rent it out. It was a two-story frame structure built about the turn of the century and it showed its age. It needed a lot of work, so in my spare time I helped my father with the repairs.

During the last two weeks we were there in May 1963, a series of events occurred that could have been only the work of supernatural forces.

One Saturday morning, we were wallpapering the kitchen when I heard someone going up the steps to the second floor. I went into the hall and tiptoed quietly after the intruder. After a cautious search of all the rooms, I was sure no one was there. How the mysterious visitor escaped perplexed me. The stairway was the only entrance to the upper rooms and all the windows were locked.

The next strange occurrence came Monday the following week. I was helping my father sweep the basement when all of a sudden I turned to see him gasping for air. He seemed to be struggling with an unseen assailant. I ran to help him but before I reached him a smashing blow on my right jaw sent me reeling against the wall. The assault ceased right then but Father and I decided we had had enough excitement for that day. We suspected a poltergeist, but fearing ridicule, we told no one and reluctantly returned the following day to complete the work.

For the rest of the week we faced many violent and disgusting problems. Tools lifted up and flew around the rooms. Other objects spun into the air and smashed windows.

Always hoping our tormentor would leave, we finished the repairs and hastened to acquire a tenant but unfortunately we never found one who would stay very long. Some were so frightened they vacated the house the same day they moved in. Others complained that something beat against the wall until the plaster cracked.

My father had to admit the house was a bad investment and he sold it—at a substantial loss. Recently I learned that the old house was among many others that had been torn down to make way for a new road. This, I hope, ended the activity of our poltergeist.

—*Phillip Lamont Council, Chester, Va.*

Spirit with a Vengeance

In a Sahuarita, Arizona, cotton camp on October 15, 1959, Robert Nabors and his friend of many years, Ben

Mitchell, dueled with .410 shotguns and Mitchell was killed. After a minor altercation, Nabors said, Mitchell had slapped him. Nabors sped to his cabin and picked up his shotgun and met Mitchell, armed with his own weapon, next to the victim's cabin (No. 17). They shot almost simultaneously, but Nabors sustained only minor injuries.

When the charge of first-degree murder was reduced to manslaughter, Nabors pled guilty and was sentenced to eight to 10 years in the Arizona state prison.

I knew these facts when I moved into Cabin No. 17 in 1963, but the deed was done and it meant nothing to me … until I began "seeing things" in the middle of the night. The first time, I awakened about midnight to see a man in a white shirt standing not far from my bed. I was alone and scared out of my wits. I managed to get my pistol and flashlight from under my pillow, but the beam of light showed the room was empty. I turned on all the lights in the two-room cabin and made a thorough search. No one was there; all the windows and doors were bolted from the inside.

The next night about the same time, the same thing happened. I awakened for no apparent reason to see the man in the white shirt lurking in my room. After the third or fourth night I was no longer alarmed, for no harm ever came to me. I saw the apparition nightly for several months, and by the time I moved in late 1963, I had begun almost to take him for granted … but I was glad to get out of Cabin No. 17.

As it happened, Robert Nabors was paroled about the time I moved out of the cabin. He later returned to the Sahuarita cotton camp and moved into the cabin his victim and I had occupied.

On November 19, 1965, Nabors was found dead in the ramshackle apartment. A .32 caliber revolver lay on the bloody floor near his body but sheriff's investigators found no cuts, bullet wounds, or powder burns on the body. No explanation could be found to account for the puddle of blood on the floor. Robbery as a motive for the killing was ruled out, for almost $100 was found in the dead man's wallet, although he had been on welfare.

Nabors' death remains a mystery … unless a vengeful ghost simply bided his time.

—*Lesta Ann Myatt, Tucson, Ariz.*

Who Lives in Vine Cottage?

"Is there a ghost in Vine Cottage, Angmering-on-Sea, Sussex, England? This question is being asked after a London couple went to view the century-old picturesque cottage in Sea Road and claimed they saw the owner—who died two years ago!"

The London couple referred to in the June 1967 item from an English newspaper is my husband and I.

We were house-hunting and had driven from London to the Sussex coast to see Vine Cottage. The estate agent's report advertised a flint-and-brick cottage with a slate roof, built in the 1860s. It had a walled garden 150 yards from the sea and had stood empty and for sale for the last 12 months. We picked up the keys from the Realtor and went along to see it.

Once inside the wrought iron gate, we found ourselves behind ivy-covered walls in a long lawn leading up to the cottage. It was a solid unadorned little place, plain and sturdy. It had been built to last, and only a Virginia creeper climbing up its front softened the squareness. We paused on the lawn, marveling at the seclusion and peace.

Suddenly my husband said, "Look at the upstairs window! It's got a curtain."

I looked up and there in the empty house I saw a white lace curtain. As we watched, it was parted and a white-haired lady wearing a grey shawl looked out at us.

Our first reaction was embarrassment. We had been told the place was empty and we now found ourselves intruding on an occupant. The figure at the window made no move to welcome us but stood staring as we retreated down the lawn and out the gate.

Up the road from the cottage is a hardware store, The Corner Ironmongers, and we went in to ask the proprietor, Mr. J. Furlong, who was living in the cottage.

"No one's living there," he said. "It's been empty for the last 12 months."

"That's what we understood," we explained, "but we've just been there and found an old lady upstairs!"

He asked what she looked like. We described her white hair and grey shawl and the strange way she stood and stared at us.

"That's Mrs. Ayling," he said. "She always wore a shawl and looked just as you've described her. But she died two years ago!" He went on to say that Mrs. Nudd Ayling had lived in the cottage for 60 years and died in 1965 at age 94.

Somehow we did not feel we wanted to go back. We returned the keys to the estate agents who reiterated that the cottage had been empty for a year. No one could have entered it and the agent had all the keys.

Mrs. Ayling's 69-year-old son is a fishmonger in nearby Rustington. When he heard our story his comment to the newspaper reporter was that he never had seen his mother's ghost nor any other. He "doesn't believe" in them.

Well, we had come from London and never had heard of the Aylings, but we saw the old lady with our own eyes. Was she trying to tell us something or simply warning us off? If it were the latter she succeeded. We are not buying Vine Cottage and so far as I know it's still for sale.

Lavinia Bradley, East Preston, Sussex, England

Spirits Helping the Living

Was it just dumb luck or was it an angelic intervention? While luck can be best described as the coincidence of things going your way at just the right moment, most people know the difference between that and having something miraculous happen. We search for explanations that sound rational but are left with the conclusion that an unseen hand has assisted us in one form or another.

The wonderful experience of divine intervention—the miracle of happenstance in the most unexpected and dire situations—is the ultimate form of enlightenment. *FATE* magazine's archives are overflowing stories from people who have been touched and enlightened by a presence from beyond the grave. These tales represent some of the most personal and touching of all the ghostly stories presented here, and will hopefully inspire others to share their experiences in the future.

The Missing Billfold

In June 1964, my daughter and her husband decided to take a trip and asked my husband and me to stay in their apartment in Los Angeles and take care of Happy, their cat.

We had been there a few days when I noticed a key in the clothespin bag hanging outside on the clothesline. I soon discovered the key fit the door to my daughter's apartment. When I asked the landlady about it, she said that my daughter and her husband often forgot their key and, since the screen door had a safety catch on it she left the key in the clothes bag for them. I felt a little nervous about leaving the key outside, but she assured me no one else knew about it.

A few days later, my husband and I went to the races at Hollywood Park and returned about 7:00 p.m. My husband was very tired and went to bed about a half hour later. When I walked into the bedroom, I noticed that he had thrown his trousers over a chair and, although his billfold containing $57 and all his personal cards were still in the pocket, I hung them up.

I slept soundly that night until about 4:00 a.m. when I heard Happy scratching at the door. After letting him out, I thought vaguely that I had forgotten to lock the door, but since the safety catch was on the screen I went back to bed.

When my husband awoke the next morning he looked for his billfold, but it wasn't in his pocket. We searched the entire apartment, even emptied all the drawers, without finding it. Eventually our young couple returned and we went back home without the billfold.

Six months later, in the following January, we attended a Spiritualist meeting. It was the usual procedure, a service and then mediums giving individual readings.

When the medium got to me, she said, "Your father is here. He says the word 'happy.' He says he saw you taking care of a cat. It is not your cat and he mentions the word 'happy' again."

"It is the name of the cat," I said.

The medium asked me whether I wanted to ask a question.

"What became of the billfold?" I inquired.

The medium replied that she received the number "57." She saw someone come in and remove the billfold during the night. But, she said, it would be returned soon with the money.

I had small hope of this since so much time had gone by. Human nature being what it is, the odds were against our ever seeing the money again, I thought.

Two days later my daughter telephoned. "I found Charlie's billfold," she announced. "It has $57 in it."

I asked her where in the world she had found it, knowing that she had given her place a complete house-cleaning soon after we left in June.

"Just a few minutes ago I went to take something out of my middle dresser drawer," she said. "When I opened it there was the billfold right in plain sight, lying on top of all my things!"

There are several lines of conjecture in regard to this mystery: the supposed thief felt some kind of pressure to make restitution, either from his own conscience or through spirit intervention; another possibility lies in the more incredible fact that I have had things simply disappear and reappear through what is called apportation. Or the explanation may be a combination of these things—the thief had no intention of returning the purse but it was apported from his (or her) possession into the drawer!

Probably we never will know what really happened.

—*Dulcie Brown, Fresno, Calif.*

I Was Afraid

I have tried to live close to God. My mother was a Christian, but she died when I was a little girl, back in Mississippi.

In 1952 I was living on Missouri Avenue, in St. Louis, Missouri, and working in a laundry to support my own daughter, as my husband and I were not together. The day at work was hard. I was tired at night. One

Wednesday evening in August I decided to go to bed early. My daughter had gone to the movies with a friend.

We lived in an old house. It seemed when you entered it as if you had gone backwards in time. Our room was on the second floor, in the rear. You had to walk down a long hall to get to it.

On this particular evening something happened to me that I never can forget. I was lying on the bed knowing deep sleep was not too far away when it occurred.

We had one window on the west side of our room and two windows on the south side. Near one of the windows was an old stove that matched the rest of the old-fashioned, out-of-date furniture. When you're poor that is the way you have to live.

Suddenly I felt like I was floating. There was a buzzing noise in my head and a rose-colored light lit up the room. From the window on the south, I saw my mother coming toward me. She reached the middle of the room, only a few feet from where I lay. I wasn't dreaming! I know what I saw!

Mother had on the same dress in which she had been buried—only the dress had changed color, now it was as white as snow; at the time of her funeral it had been pink. But it was the same dress. She had her hands folded in front of her and her eyes were open very wide, as if in fright, as if something bad was about to happen.

Then she began to speak to me.

She said, "Someone close to me, whom I love very much is about to be here with me."

She was going to tell me who it was, but I was sure she was going to say it was I and I was afraid. I began to pray to God, begging him not to let me know who it was that was going to die. (Oh, Mother, can you ever forgive me for being afraid that night?) I shouldn't have been afraid of my mother, for she loved me very much. If she ever comes again I hope I have the courage to listen to her, but that night I was afraid.

When I began to pray, saying I didn't want to know who it was, Mother started back the way she had come. She went out the window she had come in.

The following Friday my sister, who lives in Arkansas, went to church, leaving five children at home in the care of an old uncle. She took only the two oldest children to church with her. While she was gone, her house caught on fire. The babies, a set of twins only eight months old, perished in the fire; the other three children were saved.

I know Mother had come to warn me. Now I wonder over and over, if I had listened to her could I have saved my sister's babies?

I'll never know—for I was afraid of my own mother. But I do wonder, too, why Mother came to me instead of to my sister.

—Myrtle Cooper, Imperial, Mo.

My Father's Voice

Twenty-two years have passed since my father's death and, while I believe there has been evidence through the years he still was helping me, something happened in March 1963, which startled me.

I was ill and alone in Providence Hospital. My only son was half-a-world away. The doctors were certain my illness had caused serious heart damage and were sending me to the heart exercise room at 10 o'clock the next morning. Long after the nurse had given me a sedative, turned on the nightlight, and gone noiselessly away, I lay tense and unable to close my eyes. I was thinking, I was too young to retire; I am not able financially, because of frequent hospitalization, to spend long months being idle while my damaged heart heals. I was upset.

Suddenly it seemed a cool hand rested on my head. Distinctly I heard my father's voice, as I heard it often in childhood, "Sleep now, girl, everything will be all right."

The next day when the cardiograms and examinations were completed, my doctor came into my room smiling, "Not as bad as we thought! Six weeks rest when we discharge you, then back to your office."

I was back to an eight-hour day after six weeks instead of months, and have not lost a day since because of illness.

—*Louise Savage Mapp, Washington, D.C.*

Who Warned Me?

When I was a youngster, my knowledge of "strange" happenings consisted of a few little stories my mother Virgie Rioux used to tell about "table rapping." Since these experiences came from the inconceivable distance of her teenage years, I believed in nothing but facts!

We lived in Shreveport, Louisiana, in 1926, where I attended the C. E. Byrd High School. It was customary in the spring for the juniors to entertain the soon-to-be graduated seniors, and our type of fun in those days was a combination hayride and wiener roast. We planned to go to a large plantation about 15 or 20 miles north of the city and several flatbed trucks layered with hay were provided. For city kids, this was a joy in itself!

We anticipated lots of fun, but our parents may have been apprehensive. Those were Prohibition days, and along our route were quite a few "speakeasies." Where and how the illegal liquor was made was a moot point. Sometimes it caused a paralyzing illness and to say the least, "bad" liquor quickly produced a high degree of intoxication. It was to be expected that more accidents occurred on the highways harboring the speakeasies.

At any rate, we arrived at the plantation with no difficulty, roasted our wieners, yelled, joked, and raced around as teenagers do.

About 10 p.m. our leaders said it was time to start home. (Our parents had some silly idea that we had to be in by 11 p.m.—even on Fridays and Saturdays!)

Reluctantly, we took our places on the outer edges of the truckbed. My partner Joe chose the left side over the rear wheels. Why I'll never know, but had he not, this story could not have been told.

As the truck leisurely proceeded along the highway, we sang the old familiar songs, laughing and joking as only carefree kids can. Over the noise I distinctly heard a voice say, "Get your feet up!" Since we were packed in like sardines, I shrugged off the impression as we continued our homeward journey.

The second time the warning was stronger: "Get your feet UP!" But someone or something on the truck—I don't remember what—diverted my attention and again I ignored the warning.

The third warning, the same words loud and clear, was unmistakable. I asked, "Why?" and just as clearly came the answer "A car will pass and strike right here!"

Now I squirmed, trying to make room so that I could sit cross-legged, Yogi fashion. The process of getting into this position led Joe to ask if I were cold. When I said no, he pressed further, "Well, why are you sitting that way?"

I told him the truth. "A car may pass and hit here."

He chuckled and said, "Oh, no, it won't!"

Nevertheless I continued to sit cramped and cross-legged the rest of the way. More than once I glanced back along the highway and finally two headlights loomed in the distance. Vividly I can see them now, dim and close together, typical of cars of the mid-twenties.

The car rapidly closed the gap between us, with the unmistakable weaving motion of drunken driving, and sure enough, as it passed the truck, the back of the car forcefully whacked the truckbed, splintering the edge. Joe's knee was scratched and he looked at me in alarm.

"Something told you to move?" he asked. All I could do was nod my head.

Had I not been persistently warned, not once but three times, I surely would have suffered painful, even serious injury. Had I overlooked the third and most insistent warning, I might have had lots of time to ponder in a nearby hospital.

—*Dolphine Rioux Webb, Texarkana, Ark.*

Mother's Warning

On January 25, 1950, my mother, who died September 18, 1939, spoke a warning to me that undoubtedly saved my life. "Dorothy," she said, "See a doctor at once. Don't delay."

I was in the kitchen at the time, working at the sink. I had been feeling half-sick, half-well for about two months but had neglected to see a doctor, in the hope that whatever was troubling me eventually would clear up.

The sound of my mother's voice coming from behind me, outside my range of vision, didn't frighten me but I was startled. The identity of the voice was unmistakable, and I knew at once that I should heed it.

The following day I made an appointment with Dr. Hite, the family doctor, for a thorough examination. Dr. Hite determined that I was suffering from chronic appendicitis and advised an immediate operation.

Five days later I underwent surgery. The operation was none too soon. On the verge of rupturing, my appendix was enlarged to the point of contacting my liver, which it was beginning to damage.

"A few more days, or perhaps only hours," Dr. Hite told me later, "and you would have been in serious trouble."

This experience was particularly meaningful to me because my mother died from lack of medical attention. I am convinced she returned to warn me, to prevent me from experiencing a similar fate.

—*Dorothy J. Osborn, Toledo, Ohio*

I Wondered

I usually scoffed at descriptions of ghosts and spiritual or psychic phenomena and such, but one day I began to wonder.

As I walked along the sidewalk of a large city square, I was attracted by an unusually artistic display in a florist's window a short distance ahead.

As I approached the shop, I heard my name called distinctly. The sound came from behind me and I recognized my deceased mother's voice. It startled me. I stopped and turned around. At that precise moment, a car out of control climbed the sidewalk in front of me and crashed into the florist shop. Had I not stopped when I did, I would have been directly in its path.

I stood, unscathed, gazing at the wreckage and the horribly injured driver of the car.

I wondered!

—Cyril Carty, *Plainfield, Vt.*

The Man Who Cared

Twice during the last six years, my daughter's father-in-law, Paul Albino (who died of a heart attack on August 15, 1959) has appeared to my daughter Fern.

The first time occurred shortly after Paul's death when Fern herself was quite ill. She had not felt well for days but she kept going, hoping her general feeling of malaise would ease with time. One day after her husband had gone to work and her children were at school, she decided to lie down to rest. She must have dozed but suddenly became wide-awake. Across the room, sitting it the big armchair he favored was her father-in-law.

"Dad!" she said, "Dad, what are you doing back here?"

He didn't speak but smiled and nodded his head as much as to say, "All is well now." As she watched he gradually faded away.

Fern's husband laughed at her story, saying the vision of his father had been imagination, probably due to her illness. Nevertheless, she began to feel better and in a short time became her old self again.

In June 1965, Fern and her husband decided to repaint their house and this meant chipping off the old paint. They both worked hard at it every spare minute but her husband had a job to do and she had a family to care for. The work was not progressing very fast, so one afternoon she decided to put in some extra time chipping the paint. After several hours on the scaffold, she had earned a rest and went inside. Strangely, she still heard the sound of chipping. She stopped and listened; the chipping continued.

"Lloyd?" she called, thinking perhaps her husband had come home early and gone right to the chipping job. It was not her husband who answered, but her father-in-law Paul.

"It's me, Fernie," he said. "You kids are always taking on more than you can handle and I'm just going to help out a bit on this."

Fern ran to the back of the house and out the kitchen door. On her way she heard the crash of falling plaster paint. When she reached the outdoors, there at the base of the wall lay a pile of dried paint and above it a large clean place from where it had fallen. To chip that much paint by hand would have taken many hours.

—*Velma Dorrity Cloward, Modesto, Calif.*

The Bequest

I never knew my father. He was hanged for murder a few weeks before I was born. My mother would not talk to me about him and only through other relatives did I learn what he was like.

Leon Spencer, Sr., was a small-town newspaper editor who invariably took the side of the underdog in all controversies. He was considered quite eccentric. He believed that dreams were caused by the spirit leaving the body and roaming around, communing with other spirits, and that the events dreamed were actual occurrences in the spirits' lives.

In the weeks that he was imprisoned awaiting execution, my father made a will leaving our farm home near Valley Falls, South Carolina, and his interest in the newspaper to my mother, but he repeatedly refused to reveal the hiding place of any cash. To Mother's entreaties, he replied that at the proper time his spirit would let his "child" know the location.

Naturally, I had heard this story and I sincerely believed that my father some day would reveal the hiding place and that I would be rich. But the memory and the dream were growing dim by 1922 when I was 12 years old.

Then one night I was awakened by a low voice. It was soft, but it seemed to fill the room.

"Leon! Wake up. It's your father. Go into the kitchen and remove the second brick from the top row of the fireplace."

I didn't waken my mother but went to the kitchen and did as I had been told. The proper brick came out easily; the mortar was loose. Behind the brick was a hollow space. I reached in and found a metal box. It opened easily and the first thing I saw was a note which read: "For my child, from Dad." In the box was $2,000 in currency and $700 in gold coins.

—*Leon Spencer, Charleston, S.C.*

My Spiritual Surgeon

One bright August day in 1959, I was pruning the rose bushes around our Rochester, New York, home. Somehow I lost my balance and fell, striking my shoulder on a rock. I am a nurse, so I recognized a bone snap and even as I fainted I knew my arm was broken.

Later in the hospital X-rays showed 19 large fractures and small ones too numerous to count. The humerus was too badly smashed to put in a cast, so my arm was placed in a sling. It was an agonizing arrangement for the sling would slip and I could hear as well as feel the bones crunching. Even powerful morphine-derivative drugs barely took the edge off the pain. Night after sleepless night I gritted my teeth while the doctor's words burned into my brain. "You'll never work again," Dr. Kenneth Cooley, an orthopedic specialist had told me, "because you'll never be able to raise your arm nor clasp your hands behind your back. In your case, physical therapy is not the answer, but in a week you must start exercising your arm."

Soon I was exercising and groaning and weeping with the pain of it. My family encouraged me to persist, but my spirits were low. I reflected that even my piano playing days were over, and music always had meant a great deal to me.

One hot night I dozed off—only to be awakened by a voice saying, "Don't be frightened. I am a spirit surgeon. You have suffered long enough and needlessly. I wish to operate on your arm. I can put those smashed bones together."

I was wide awake! The moon shone through the blinds and I clearly saw the now familiar hospital room. I felt no fear—only trust and confidence as I looked into this man's kind face. He wore rimless glasses over bright brown eyes and he had a thick brown beard. I particularly noticed the celluloid collar and cuffs of another day and his old fashioned white surgical coat.

"You will feel no pain," he assured me. "I'll put you to sleep. But you must discontinue your exercises for 10 days or this operation will not succeed." Speechless, I nodded my agreement.

When next I awakened it was daylight. I had had hours of refreshing sleep, flat on my back. My arm felt stiff and sore and now was bound in an Ace bandage within the sling. (An Ace is a long narrow elastic bandage mostly used to bind sprains and broken bones.) I now felt no need for the painkillers I had been taking.

When I tried to explain the visitation and midnight operation to my husband, he laughed at me but my refusal to exercise upset him. He explained away the Ace bandage by saying I had put it on in my sleep, although he must have known this would have been impossible.

Stubbornly, I resisted my family's pleas to exercise and tried not to be hurt by their outspoken idea that I was "fey."

On the tenth day my daughter took off the Ace bandage. We looked for scars on my shoulder but there were none. Thus the family had further cause for kidding me about "my dream."

Five weeks later, my husband took me to Dr. Cooley's office for my final checkup and release from the hospital. My arm hung straight at my side. The doctor stared, then came around from behind his desk for a closer look. I raised my arm and patted the top of my head and as he registered sheer astonishment I turned and clasped my hands behind my back. Wordlessly he put my arm in every conceivable position, growing more and more amazed.

"Get her X-rays," he snapped to his nurse.

He studied the pictures carefully and then spoke in awe.

"Believe me, Alicia, your healing is unbelievable. I call it a miracle. That arm, by all medical knowledge, should be stiff and useless."

"I play the piano, too," I gloated.

He sighed, "I wish I could take credit for it. I'm good, but no one could repair that much damage except someone up there." He pointed skyward.

The absence of scars puzzled me until one day while dressing in front of the mirror I plainly saw the scars of surgical clamps in a row from my shoulder almost to the elbow. They remain visible today as proof of the medical skill of a spirit surgeon.

—*Alicia Mason, Miami Beach, Fla.*

A Friend in Need

Met Acey-Acey Callaghan in a little gin mill off Fremont in Las Vegas, Nevada, in 1946. I had been bucking the dice and as usual had lost my weekend allowance. Acey-Acey had been watching me. Now he introduced himself and started to tell me what it was I had been doing wrong.

He was a pro and he taught me things about odds and percentages I never had dreamed of. Later he took me to his room at El Rancho Vegas and taught me more.

One of the things he said was never to back the two—the double ace. (Odds are 35 to one against you and the house pays off only 29 to one.) He said when he was young and ignorant he had kept himself broke making that bet and that was how he acquired his nickname, "Acey-Acey."

We became friends, and for some time I saw him every time I visited Vegas, which was just about every week. Then for no particular reason, our meetings became less frequent and finally ceased altogether.

I always gambled for fun but there came a time—the winter of 1950—when I desperately needed a lot of money in a hurry. Gambling was the only way I could think of to get it. I took my small stake and hit the carpet joints on the Strip.

Naturally I lost. I was actually down to my last dollar chip—and then something strange happened. My depression lifted and I felt as if I could take the world. I looked around and there was Acey-Acey.

"Shoot the double ace," he said.

Without hesitation I made the bet and it hit. I had $30.

"Press it all the way," Acey-Acey said.

I did and it hit again. I picked up my $900 in chips and went to cash them in. I looked around for Acey-Acey but didn't see him. Thinking perhaps he had a mad on because hadn't dropped around for so long went to El Rancho Vegas, determined to apologize and thank him.

The desk clerk there told me Acey-Acey had been buried two weeks before.

—Gene R. Cannady, Torrance, Calif.

Animal Spirits

Our friends and our loved ones can often encompass more than just the blood relations commonly regarded as "family." Sometimes the bonds of love transcend the typical to a higher place where the connection between man and animal is purely spiritual. Dogs, cats, and horses have lived side by side with human beings since we discovered that we all get along together rather well. Since then, we have given them names as we would our children, rejoiced in the happiness they bring us, and weep at their all-too-soon passing. And as we mourn for them, are they not capable of feeling the loss of camaraderie in our passing as well? If people are capable of becoming ghostly apparitions or angelic harbingers that hold on to the edge of life with purpose, then why not our animal companions, too?

And perhaps this is why our animal friends have stayed close and watched over us even in their death. An eternal bond that can only be described in the love we feel for those furry friends that cannot speak, but say so much in the most subtle of ways.

The story of a life saved from fire by a faithful dog and a mule that seemed to possess an intelligence greater than one could expect compose just some of the readers' letters found in this chapter. Real stories that will make you feel good knowing that we may be reunited with more than just family and friends in the afterlife.

Phantom Stallion

In 1913 I lived with my husband on a ranch near Calgary, Alberta, Canada.

I often drove to Calgary in a carriage pulled by Billy, my grey horse. Billy was alert and intelligent; when we traveled about in Calgary, Billy would stop by himself and let the streetcar go by when no one got off, but if the bell rang he knew he could cross over.

When Billy was harnessed to the carriage, he always looked to see what my husband and I were taking. If two big cream cans were in the front of the carriage, he took the road to the creamery. If there were no cans he took the other road to my brother's wife's home in the hills. Billy never made a mistake.

One time he saved my life.

I was driving home after visiting by brother's wife. The Central Pacific Railroad had made a cut through a hill to give them a shorter route to the city of Calgary. I had to drive into this narrow cut to get home to our ranch.

One time, when the rocky road was frozen and the wheels of my carriage made a very loud noise, I did not hear the bell. But Billy did and stopped short. I told him to go on. He turned his head and gave me a very peculiar look. He would not move. Just then the Central Pacific Railroad flyer came rushing past. If we had been in the middle of that opening, we would have been smashed.

Another memorable experience I had with Billy seemed to indicate that he was psychic. While I was driving to Calgary with Billy on a day in 1913, a shipment of stallions arrived at a railway siding about two miles from the ranch of John Turner, the man who had bought them.

He imported stallions from Scotland to sell to Alberta farmers. The stallions had to be walked to the Turner Ranch, each horse being led by one man. About halfway to the ranch one of the stallions had become sick and died. He was buried in Dr. McKid's pasture near a gate.

A few hours later, I was driving back home in the dusk. When we passed the gate where the stallion had been buried, Billy stopped suddenly and whistled, as though he saw another horse.

Billy stood still for a few seconds, then stepped over to the left side of the road, as if to make room for another horse. Billy was very friendly with this invisible creature. He leaned over and rubbed against something and whinnied gently.

Then Billy started to pull the carriage. I had the strange feeling I was driving a team of horses because the carriage rocked from one side to the other. After I drove like this for about a mile, the rocking suddenly stopped, as though the stallion had left. Billy whistled, as if saying "goodbye" and moved back to the right, toward the center of the road.

As we continued homeward, I wondered what Billy had seen. I had the eerie feeling he had seen the ghost of the stallion.

—*Mary H. Williamson, Los Angeles, Calif.*

Old Butch

One afternoon in November 1952, I was hiking back to my car after a day of hunting when I sensed something was lying in the brush.

Upon investigating, I found a gray English bulldog that had been shot through the neck, probably by some hunter too careless to identify his targets.

At the time, my only thought was to carry him back to the car and give him a decent burial. It turned out, however, that the animal wasn't dead, for his feebly wagging tail indicated that he was grateful for my assistance.

Butch, as I called him for lack of a better name, had been very lucky. The bullet had passed completely through his throat without causing serious damage. A week later I had him back on his feet. The only permanent injury was to his voice, which made him bark with a distinctive croak.

Several newspaper ads failed to locate Butch's owner, so I then decided to keep him. In 10 years, I never regretted this decision nor do I think Butch ever had a regret either.

He always seemed perfectly happy to curl up in his corner and watch me as I worked.

One night in 1962, death crept up on Butch and carried him away. It was a very gentle death; there was not a sound. Even after it was over, his eyes were still upon me in that protective gaze I knew so well.

Over a year later and 1,000 miles from that spot, I awoke in the middle of the night to hear Butch's unmistakable croak. When I got up to investigate, I found the hall outside my bedroom filled with smoke. I ran outside of the house and it burst into flames.

People thought it a miracle that I had awakened and escaped from the fire.

As I stood in the cold street watching the last of my house go up in flames, tears filled my eyes as I thought of my old friend. Old Butch was still watching over me with his protective gaze.

—*David Antler, Horseheads, N.Y.*

A Jerked Coverlet

I am not a Spiritualist. I have not studied Spiritualism. My only knowledge of it came as a child when I watched séances conducted by my grandmother, Lena Puerner, who was considered an excellent medium. The séances frightened me; I was too young to understand.

Apparently a lack of knowledge of Spiritualism is no barrier to participating in mediumistic experiences. Some years ago I visited two friends in Highland Park, Illinois, Mrs. Joan Korhumel and her daughter, Dorothy. They both were ardent Spiritualists.

The night of my visit, Dorothy suggested that I sleep in her room and that she and her mother would occupy the master bedroom.

I was very tired and went sound asleep immediately. Just before dawn, I was awakened when the coverlet was pulled off my bed. It was a warm night, but I was chilled and frightened. I satisfied myself that no one was in the room, mentally kicked myself for being a fool, picked up the coverlet, and went back to sleep.

It was a short sleep. The coverlet was again pulled off the bed and lay on the floor. My chills and fright returned. But dawn was breaking and the faint light filtering through the window indicated that no one was in the room with me. Puzzled, but reassured, I finally dozed.

Another sharp tug woke me to find the coverlet on the floor again! This time I did not go back to sleep and I waited until I heard Dorothy and her mother tiptoe down to the first floor to get breakfast.

A little hesitantly I related my experience with the coverlet at breakfast. I don't know what reaction I expected from Dorothy and her mother, but I was not prepared for the peculiar look I saw on each of their faces. They started to speak, then hesitated; finally Dorothy blurted, "It would happen to you!"

"What do you mean," I asked.

"Well, here Mother and I have been hoping for a materialization and it happened to you. And you're not even a Spiritualist!"

"Do you think I experienced the materialization of someone?" I asked.

"It wasn't a person," Dorothy answered, "but I had two dogs who passed away and each morning at dawn they would wake me by pulling the cover off my bed— and you were sleeping in my room!"

—Mildred A. Puerner, Chicago, Ill.

Dogs from Nowhere

My parents moved to Hollywood, a suburb of Spokane, Washington, in 1908, when I was eight years old. There was no running water, electricity, or gas, and we had kerosene lamps and a wood- and coal-burning stove in the kitchen. Pine trees and wild flowers grew all around our house.

The Northwest Boulevard ran along the edge of the meadow that fronted the house. On the other side of the road was a steep embankment, below which the Spokane River flowed deep and treacherous.

My parents had forbidden me to go near the river, but early one morning in June I opened the screen in my bedroom window, jumped out, and headed for the river. I felt sure I would be able to return before the household was awake. Dawn was just breaking, and I made good time over the bank and down to the river. A driveway ran alongside the river and by keeping on the driveway I felt I was obeying the letter of the law, if not the spirit.

Before long, I heard a crashing in the underbrush and two large dogs came out and joined me on my walk. One looked part collie; the other was as nondescript as most of the dogs the local ranchers used to drive their sheep to market. They frisked about and, as by this time I was a little frightened at being so alone, I was glad to have their company.

Eventually I came to a wooden bridge that spanned the river. The bridge led from Fort George Wright some-where across the river and continued on my side until it joined the Boulevard. Crossing the bridge from the Fort side came a most disreputable looking man, dirty and ragged. Instinctively I seemed to be warned.

I tried to hide in the bushes beside the road, but he saw me and headed straight for my hiding place. By this time I was terrified. I could see the evil leer on his face, and I screamed as he reached out to clutch me.

In an instant, both dogs were at my side. The collie snarled and jumped at the tramp. The other dog circled him with low growls, hackles bristling, but did not attack.

The tramp drew a knife from his pocket—I could hear the click and see the sun flash on the steel.

He slashed the collie across the muzzle, a great deep cut. The dog howled in pain, but fastened his teeth in the tramp's shirt as the other dog went into action and knocked the man down. All I could see was a flurry of dogs, flailing arms and legs, and blood all over.

I ran, and when I stopped to look back I saw the tramp running back across the bridge with both dogs in pursuit. When I reached the Boulevard, I called the dogs, but they did not come. I had blood all over my torn dress and was a sorry sight as I trudged on up the Boulevard until I came to a meadow.

There was a wagon and a herd of sheep grazing in the field and an Indian family gathered around something on the ground. They had come from Nine Mile Road, which was in a different direction. As I approached, the group separated. There lay my two dogs, stiff and cold upon the ground.

I began to cry, believing the dogs had been mortally hurt protecting me in the fracas with the tramp. The Indian father asked why I was crying. When I told him the two dogs had fought off a tramp who had tried to harm me, the whole family stared in disbelief. One of the little boys told me the dogs had eaten poisoned coyote bait and died very early that morning on the way to Spokane for treatment.

Yet, I knew they were the same dogs. Across the muzzle of the collie was a deep knife slash and blood was still caked around his mouth.

The old Indian father took my hand and gazed at me for a long time without speaking. Finally he said he believed me, even though he knew the dogs had been dead. He said the Great Spirit had taken care of me.

When I got home, my parents were frantic with worry, and the neighbors were preparing to search for me. I told my parents what I had done, and that two dogs had rescued me. But I never told the rest of the story. I shall always feel that the dogs were sent to me from Heaven and that I owe my life to their guardianship.

—*Wilma Richardson, San Bernardino, Calif.*

Hair of the Dog that Haunted Us

Animal visitations, wizardry, and witchcraft are not confined to medieval parchment. That such forces can and do occasionally penetrate the gauze surrounding our prosaic world my wife and I testify from personal experience. Once, for many nerve-wracking months we unwillingly shared our apartment with such an entity.

Our beast showed us nothing but chilling malevolence during its short periods of materialization as well as during those times when it prowled, heard but unseen, just beyond focus of human sight, advising us of its presence by low throaty growls or threatening us with sounds of snapping teeth and loud breathing. Sometimes heavy objects were hurled at us with, fortunately, greater force than accuracy. Our daemon, unlike others, either deliberately or inadvertently bequeathed us lasting proof of its powers of materialization.

Before me as I write is a glossy hair with six definite waves in its 10-inch length. Heavy and coarse, it does not have the quality of human hair. Even today, more than 20 years later, it is impossible for me to view this hair without feeling again something of the shock that numbed me the evening I first encountered the materialized, snarling, vicious beast from whose shaggy, black coat this and two similar hairs came into my possession.

Before the end of World War II, mustered out of the service because of war-incurred, partial disability, I returned to the Los Angeles area with my wife to find close friends had dispersed and permanent housing was impossible to find. Even rooming house accommodations were unobtainable. Hotel rooms could be rented on a 24-hour basis only. Consequently, we moved from place to place for eight weeks until my wife, despite a naturally optimistic nature, began to react unfavorably to the strain, possibly because she was four-months pregnant with our first child.

Then, unexpectedly, we found the apartment we occupied for the next several years. Accurately speaking, we were not led to the apartment so much as it seemed led to us. One day I was in the office of Cyril Stuart, supervisor of the small plant where I worked, when his telephone rang. After hanging up, he jocularly asked if I could recommend a quiet couple for an apartment just vacated. He had no idea we were at rope's end in our search for living quarters. It developed that his wife managed an eight-unit building off of Beverly Boulevard, within shouting distance of the Doheny Drive boundary line of fashionable Beverly Hills. I tried to give him a deposit on the spot, but he insisted I see the apartment and discuss the lease with Mrs. Stuart.

Early the following day my wife, Lani, and I found the address to be a squarish, white stucco building with Spanish tile roofing. It had been built in 1915. The available apartment was fairly spacious, with rounded ceilings and Spanish arches. Door and occasional paneling were of beautiful, rubbed eucalyptus wood. A kitchen, dining room, bath, and bedroom, furnished, with utilities, could be rented for $45 a month! We hurriedly signed the lease, after which we checked the inventory, deposited the initial rent, and went off happily to the Bekins' warehouse to arrange for our furniture to be released from storage and delivered, if possible, that afternoon.

Some months later, Lani and I admitted to each other that during that first inspection of the apartment we had sensed an unpleasant atmosphere—a guttering of the exuberance we originally had felt. Although brilliant sunshine had flooded the rooms, we each had been aware of a clammy dampness, something penetrating enough to be disturbing.

It should be stated that for many years prior to these specific hauntings, Lani and I had investigated psychic phenomena and had learned to catalog them unemotionally in order to maintain a valid journal. We know that memory cannot be depended upon.

Our belongings were delivered late that afternoon and by evening we were exhausted from carrying the original apartment furniture to the basement. With relief we relaxed, tired and happy, in the midst of the crated litter. Our grand piano stood in the center of the living room surrounded by barrels and cartons containing the beloved accumulation we had put in storage before the war. I broke open a crate of books. At one side of the room was a Spanish-type fireplace whose high mantle, six feet from the floor, was a shelf 15 inches wide. On this set a dozen or so of the larger volumes, wedging them tightly together against the chimney wall, leaving a margin of about seven inches between the books and the front edge of the shelf. Then I sank into a chair beside Lani. We regarded the high mantel with its expanse of stucco wall above and remarked that it was the perfect spot for a large oil painting that now leaned, crated, against one of the walls.

These words scarcely had died away when a heavy book, a 2-inch thick 8 by 10 tome, left its position on the mantel and, without disturbing any of the volumes flanking it on either side, flew directly at me—a distance of 15 feet through the air! At the same time there was a sharp report from the center of the room. I leaped sideways out of my chair as the book struck the floor where my feet had been. With this characteristic overture, our poltergeist commenced the hostilities that were to endure for almost a year.

At first, we were interested and curious as we faithfully kept the daily journal of inexplicable events, which had not yet begun to terrify or affect us with an almost hypnotic depression.

With one exception, the other tenants refused to visit our apartment for more than a few minutes at a time. Each felt something there that they could not understand, or they had listened to too many former, lease-breaking tenants.

As time passed, we learned to accept the foggy outlines of people and animals that appeared with the illusive yet unmistakable density of heavy mist. Many times these were accompanied by disturbing vibrations that left us overcome with melancholy. One afternoon a neighbor woman, in the midst of casual conversation, burst into deep sobbing for no reason that could be explained, except by her statement that this same emotion, a profound grief had come upon her on two former occasions when she had entered the apartment to visit other occupants.

Reviewed from the distance of 20 years, we realize how perilously close to disaster we came by way of our own neurotic reactions. We seem to have believed that a sort of intuitive truce existed between us and it; that if we ignored it, it would not harm us. However, eventually, I telephoned for an appointment with the Monseigneur of a nearby diocese. But, unfortunately, he was too sensible to embrace a truth that his church has known for centuries. I was dismissed with abrupt impatience. Apparently he believed me capable of a rather low form of practical joke.

My next questions were directed to a medical doctor, who brushed me and the topic aside with the curt reminder that many women are emotionally unstable during pregnancy, at which times husbands—I in particular—often assume these moods with psychosomatic sympathy.

But, obviously, this did not explain why visiting friends had the same eerie experiences.

Eleanor Gates, the novelist and playwright, spent an occasional weekend with us. She was a remarkable psychic who for years had investigated poltergeist activity and allied disturbances in most of the English-speaking countries. She saw our beast at night on several occasions long before I did. She identified it as a large dog in which she believed the earthbound consciousness of a murderer was trapped. She attempted an exorcism, but this failed.

There is not space in this account in detail the small persecutions we endured during those months—a handkerchief or a book jerked from our fingers, articles vanishing only to reappear the next instant in some improbable location across the room. Although neither Lani nor I are religious in the orthodox sense, we felt that whatever it was needed great understanding and help, which we, in our ignorance, were unable to give.

In due course our daughter was born. When Lani and the baby returned from the hospital, we felt that for the time being, at least, we would be comparatively free from intraworld annoyance. Rightly or not, we believe infants carry their own protection, and for a time this seemed to be true.

Then one evening when Lani and I sat quietly reading in the living room, suddenly from above and behind me something shot downward from the center of the rounded ceiling, an expanse of plain, white plaster without fixture or chandelier. I felt the wind of its passing—felt my hair move as it grazed my left temple. My instinctive sideways lurch would not have saved me had the missile been thrown with greater accuracy.

A pair of needle-sharp, eight-inch, nickel-plated scissors hit the top of a low record cabinet two feet from us, striking with sufficient force to splinter a deep furrow in the hardwood. There was no normal bounce; they struck sharply, rose straight up about six inches, then came to rest on the cabinet surface with soundless gentleness.

Neither of us ever had seen the scissors before that moment, nor did we ever discover where they came from. But their advent heralded the renewal of hostilities from our unwelcome intruders.

The first time we needed a babysitter, we had to engage one from some distance away. The neighborhood wives flatly refused to spend any time in our apartment. The recommended, matronly woman who sat for us that first evening never had heard of us nor our ghostly problems, yet when we returned after a few hours, she was on the verge of hysterics. She was huddled in a chair in a corner of the dining area away from a spot near the fireplace where, she said, dark formless shapes had danced, weaving back and forth against the white stucco wall.

Next we employed a young married couple who welcomed the opportunity of an entire evening exploring our library of classical recordings. They seemed to be two healthy extroverts, so when we came home we were surprised to find the wife in tears and the husband trying futilely to calm her. They told us they had been seated on the floor sorting through a pile of albums when the wife, attracted by movement near the fireplace, looked up to see a partially materialized man, ugly and threatening, watching her from beside the high mantel. After this, we refused to impose upon anyone else.

Lani's spells of sudden, unreasonable anger and melancholy, so unlike her, were increasing in incidence and depth. This and my own heightened alarm urged us to exert every effort to locate other quarters. But we searched without success.

In the meantime, I tried to learn something of the building's early history. I was unable to locate anyone who remembered further back than 10 or 15 years. The nearest police station had no record against the building. I finally located a man who had lived in one of the upper apartments many years before. He told us that from about 1918 through the early 1920s, the building had been headquarters for some gangsters engaged in everything from running illegal alcohol to murder on demand and that he, himself, had worked for them in a minor capacity. At that time, the apartment house had been isolated ideally for their purposes—situated in the midst of farmland. Our informant hinted at merciless methods for extracting information and at kangaroo justice. Presumably more than one unfortunate man had met death at this address.

I wish I could substantiate this man's account but I can't; it is not proof of anything! Readers of *FATE* undoubtedly will have their own ideas about what combination of circumstances is necessary for ghosts to be seen and heard. Many persons believe the needed power is drawn from living people who unwittingly act as batteries. I hesitate before asserting anything definite apart from remarking that the evening I first encountered the beast in all its solid menace seemed no different from any other. If our intruder received its sudden surge of power from either Lani or me, we were unaware of it.

On this particular night, dark had fallen early and a cold mid-winter wind shook the palm fronds into noisy rustling. At 28 minutes after seven, I was sitting, relaxed, on a couch in the dining area where I could look into the kitchen and watch Lani baking cookies. We were talking back and forth when, all at once, the rooms echoed with a strange, prolonged cry that seemed to originate in the dressing alcove. Even before the sound died away, I realized it had not come from the baby. It can best be described, in hackneyed terms, as the wail of a lost soul—a blend of hatred, anger, agony, and supplication. A drawn-out, bubbling scream to paralyze the listener's mind.

Lani froze in the act of removing a sheet of cookies from the hot oven, unaware that she was burning her hands. Instantly I was on my feet, moving toward the living room.

For reasons easily understood, after dusk we always kept the rooms brightly lit, so that what I now saw was not the effect of shadow or uncertain lighting. I had taken several strides into the room before seeing that the deep Spanish arch leading to the hall was blocked by a glossy, jet-black animal. Long-furred, heavyset, it resembled a bear but, unlike a bear, this beast's withers, three feet from the floor, were higher than its rump. One moment it was not there! In a fraction of the next instant it materialized, swifter than the speed of a camera shutter.

Here before me was the full manifestation of a thing that, until now, I had seen only as shadowy fog against the walls.

It bulked large in the center of the arch with its body pointed down-hall, toward the alcove. It's head, held at an acute three-quarter angle, could not turn quite far enough to face me directly, but the iridescent pupils of its eyes glared balefully at me. Lips drawn menacingly back in a savage snarl showed gleaming, pointed teeth. The end of the wet red tongue curled upward, like the crest of a small crimson wave, between long, terrible, fangs. I was aware of the low, warning growl we had grown used to hearing.

As I watched, immobilized in mid-stride, it swung its head forward in line with its body, ears pricked in an attitude of eager, attentive listening. Then, resuming its original position, head pressed tightly against its left shoulder, with a last, menacing display of teeth, it vanished instantaneously, as it had appeared.

I did not move! But I remained staring at the now-empty arch! The apparition was burned into my memory—the sheen of the pelt, the hackles standing like a ruff on the neck, the 10-inch long, wavy fur lying halfway to the floor below belly; the head, the shape of the ears, the blunt snout resembling that of a chow dog. It seemed to be some frightening hybrid, a dog somehow bred to a swine or bear. Try as I might, I never was able to describe its tail, nor have I any memory of its feet, although I am sure it had some. Perhaps fear narrowed my field of observation.

After a few moments, I forced myself to walk through the now empty arch. With every cautious step, I expected to collide with that terrible thing which, although now invisible, must still occupy space somewhere.

The baby was peacefully asleep. When I returned to the kitchen Lani accepted my explanation that the baby apparently had a bad dream. She was rubbing butter on her burned hands, which now had started to blister.

I did not mention what I had seen, but I did write a full, detailed account while it was undistorted by time.

The next evening when I returned from work Lani, who is extraordinarily aware of the importance of the insignificant, told me that when she first looked in on the baby that morning she had found three coarse, jet-black, wavy hairs clutched in the infant's hand. All day she had pondered over the minor mystery of where these hairs had come from.

No outsider had been in the apartment for almost two weeks. Hardwood floors and rugs were constantly polished and vacuumed. Pillows and comforters were down-filled. There was nothing in the entire apartment, either furniture or cushions, with horsehair stuffing.

Even before I saw the hairs, I knew they would be glossy black, about 10 inches long, and wavy. At this point I told Lani my experience of the previous evening.

Carefully I put the three hairs in a plain white envelope and placed it between pages 80 and 81 of a book. The book I put on the top shelf of a cupboard at the end of the hall where it reposed undisturbed, by human agency at least, until 16 evenings later when Jascha and Franke Harling dined with us.

Franke's early musical studies had led him to many out-of-the way villages in Europe, and I was not afraid of ridicule in telling them of my encounter with the animal. When they asked to examine the hairs, I carried the book to the dining table, opened the envelope and found two hairs. To assure myself the missing strand was nowhere in the envelope I took it completely apart. I leafed through the book, page by page. Then I searched the cupboard shelf. The hair was nowhere and I suspected this third, missing hair had been dematerialized, perhaps returned to it's spectral host. Bizarre? No more so than the initial appearance of the hairs!

Several days after this a letter from my older brother, Raymond, in Vancouver, Canada, described his recent fears for our safety against powerful forces even now closing in upon us.

He wrote, "Even from here I am afraid of the terrible vibrations in your apartment."

I still have that letter.

My brother was a man of rare psychic ability and knowledge who, under usual circumstances, would have been my first confidant but for 18 months he had balanced precariously between life and death, in and out of hospital, the victim of the heart ailment that eventually killed him in 1957. In deference to this condition, we had avoided mentioning to him things of an exciting nature, especially the unusual events in our apartment.

The real surprise in his letter, however, was that he had persuaded his doctor to permit an emergency visit to us in Los Angeles.

He arrived sick and weary several days later at 1 o'clock in the morning. I made him lie down at once on the "Murphy" bed in the living room. After only a few brief sentences and the assurance that he had everything needed for a quiet rest, I retired. At no time did we mention his fears or our worrisome hauntings. By tacit consent we left these things for daylight discussion.

In the morning when I arose, shortly before 6:00 a.m., I found him seated in a chair haggard, red-eyed, and gaunt. For a moment I thought he had suffered an attack, but his first sentence told me otherwise.

"Do you know you have an animal in this apartment? A shaggy, black beast about the size of a bear? It's an evil thing with a snout like a swine. I thought I dreamed at first but it continued to snuff me the darkness. I pretended to be asleep until I could 'see' it. Then I got up, turned on the lights and all night I've been combating it. I'll tell you one thing! It'll never come back here!"

I told him of all the strange things that had occurred in the apartment and, when speaking of the hairs, added that there were now only two, since the third unaccountably had vanished. While talking, I got the book from the cupboard. Between pages 80 and 81 lay the second business envelope I had used to hold the two hairs. It contained one solitary strand!

Did some unknown force permit the beast to recover only one hair at a time? Or more frightening, had the hairs been left deliberately as part of some future intention?

"Hang onto this one," my brother said, "for curiosity sake. I doubt if there are many such pieces of 'evidence' to be found in our world. And don't worry I'll stake my life on it—this one won't disappear!"

He was right. The animal did not return either as sound, sight, or shadowy fog, although we continued to sense other presences and to see other misty forms for the remainder of our tenancy.

Yesteryear's mysteries usually become today's science, and the past 20 years gradually have encouraged a universal exploration of many unknown realms, both physical and psychic. Today scientists are banding together in a sincere attempt to understand and control those forces loosely grouped under the heading extrasensory perception, even hoping eventually to use them as means of communication with astronauts.

A few months ago it was suggested that I permit a complete analysis and carbon 14 test to be made of the remaining hair. Naturally I am eager for a report from qualified authorities; my hesitation is that I have been advised the process may destroy the hair.

—*Hal V. de Ganges*

Just Horsing Around?

I was raised by my Aunt Mary Hicks, since my mother died before I was two years old. Just the two of us lived there in an old, old farmhouse, out of La Follette, Tennessee. Ghosts were the last thing we thought about, I assure you.

On a rainy summer night nearly 30 years ago, when I was 11 or 12 years old, we had gone to bed as usual, around dark. In those days, country folk didn't burn kerosene to make a light when sleeping was cheaper. About 10 o'clock, we were awakened by a horse. Not a horse in the house, but one walking around outside. Walking and snorting!

We lay waiting for the horse to go away. There were flowers in the front yard and we knew the horse was trampling them. But it wouldn't go away, just kept snorting and stomping real close to the house.

Finally, I went outside to chase it away but found nothing to chase. There was no horse anywhere around the house. It was dark, of course, but not too dark to see a large animal. I thought it had wandered off while I was getting outside. I looked around a little, then went back to the house.

A few minutes later, with a snort and a stomp, the old horse was back. Again I went outside—again no horse! This time I didn't look so long for I was beginning to think something wasn't quite right. This horse noise kept up for the next two hours or so, then all was quiet for the rest of the night.

Bright and early the next morning, we went out to see how much damage our "guest" had done. Nowhere around the house, front or back, was there a horse track, or so much as a broken blade of grass.

Several times in the years that followed we heard these same noises, but never were able to find a track or sign of any horse.

When I was about 18, we moved out of that house and my uncle, who had lived there as a boy, moved in.

I once asked him if he ever heard any strange noises at night.

"No," he answered, "I've never heard any queer noises, that I can think of."

"You mean," I asked, "you have never heard a horse at night?"

"Oh, that," he smiled. "I've heard that horse all my life. One stormy night, about 1840, a man riding a horse was killed by lightning on top of that ridge. Since then, on some stormy nights, the horse has been hunting his master. He probably will from now on, but it don't bother me none!"

—Jesse L. Hicks, La Follette, Tenn.

Do Animals Have Souls?

The North American Indians used to believe that each object and creature in nature had a soul. The corn, the bear, the pine tree, the foaming cataract—each was inhabited by its own individual spirit. This beautiful doctrine was crushed by the harsh assertion of Christianity that man alone possesses a soul. My experience with my favorite cat has convinced me that this tenet of Christianity is faulty and the red men of old were right.

My cat Bill, a solid silver-grey in color, was born in 1953 in this house in Port Colborne where we still live. He was the sole survivor of four offspring of a stray who hung around our house. Bill and I were close, and in the summer of 1954 he took to sleeping with me on my porch bed or in my bedroom in cold weather. I grew very fond of him and felt terrible when he died in 1955 of infection that set into wounds he suffered during his inevitable tomcatting around.

Now we have another cat, Sam, obtained as a kitten in 1958. He is a big cat, much larger and heavier than Bill was, and much darker in color.

The night of February 4, 1966, I slowly awakened in my bedroom to the realization that a heavy weight rested on my chest. I knew it was an animal because of its warmth, and I felt its small padded feet on my ribs. I opened my eyes expecting to see Sam, although as a rule Sam spent the night outdoors. To my utter amazement, the cat on my chest was Bill! I could not mistake his silvery-grey fur in the light of the full moon shining through the window. Bill stepped up to the pillow, then back across my body, but as I reached for him, he vanished.

At breakfast I told my parents about seeing old Bill. Dad merely smiled and told me that for many years he has had glimpses of a medium-sized silver-grey cat running around the property. He said he had seen it so often that he had not considered it important enough to mention.

Is it possible that a cat with such an amazing resemblance to old Bill (whose color really is not common) occasionally just happens to wander near our house? If that is the case, how did he come to seek me out that one time in my bedroom, a place familiar to Bill?

I say that the wraith-like cat my father has seen and who came to pay his respects to me is the spirit of old Bill.

—Joseph E. Suthren, Port Colborne, Ontario, Canada

The Little Stray

In the hottest part of the 1928 summer, the little stray had been seeking a home in our Seattle neighborhood for more than a week—a strange little dog of indeterminate breed, his black and white fur thin and ragged, his tail droopy and disjointed. No one wanted him. He had been yelled at and chased from every house on the street.

One day I found him lying in a tangle of dried vines in my yard. I stooped over and patted his head. He licked my hand and beat his poor abused tail against the ground.

I went into the house to bring him some food—a slice of bread, a chunk of meat and a bowl of milk.

My cat "Pick" followed. She normally is terrified of dogs, but she showed not the slightest fear of this one. As he rose, trembling to his feet to eat a shred of the meat and lap a few drops of milk, she stood close and watched him curiously. He nudged her once with his nose as if in greeting and she neither spat nor ran.

As the dog pretended to eat, as if more from politeness than any real hunger, I began to see an aura of white light around him. The light had nothing in common with the day's bright sunshine. It was as white as fog or mist or falling snow. It grew and spread until the dog, the cat, and I were standing in a vaulted chamber of white shimmering light. The atmosphere was oddly peaceful and I felt a strange exaltation. Slowly the light began to fade until only the glow of the sun was left—bright, but yellow after the whiteness that I had seen and felt.

I patted the dog again and "Pick" and I went back into the house. When I started for the corner grocery store 15 minutes later, the shabby little animal was gone. I never saw him again.

I like to believe that the little stray was an entity from a higher plane who came to this grim earth in the shape of an unlovely beast to see if any human being would show him kindness.

—*Irma Classen, Long Beach, Calif.*

Chummy is Waiting

Is there survival after death for our beloved pets? I know the answer. They go on to a fuller richer life. My little dog proved it.

In the early Sixties, the tragedy of my husband's impending death darkened our lives. Perhaps his was a more philosophical turn of mind, but he took it better than I did. He bought me a Pomeranian puppy, a rare all-black one, and he said, "He will be your pal and companion when I'm gone." I named the puppy "Chum," and after Jim died in December 1962, the little dog seemed to try with all his might to ease the long, lonely hours. We soon were inseparable and my friends, knowing my fondness for the little animal, included him in their invitations so I never had to drive alone. We traveled thousands of miles together. He was a protector and friend.

Among his endearing characteristics was his love for snow (always plentiful during our Rochester, New York, winters). He would make tunnels in the drifts and frolic around until his coal-black coat turned frosty-gray.

Shortly after my sister and I moved to Florida, Chummy took sick and despite an expert veterinarian's care, he died. The date was Sunday, February 13, 1966.

My sister was hospitalized at this time and quite ill. She loved the little dog so much that I didn't want to tell her about his death until she was better. Imagine my surprise when she telephoned me a few hours after his death. Weeping bitterly, she asked, "What time did Chummy die?"

"How did you know?" I gasped.

Her daughter Patty Patterson had telephoned from Rochester, and said Mrs. Grant, a neighbor, had asked when we got home.

Patty replied, "They aren't home. Mother is in the hospital and couldn't possibly travel."

"Well, they're home now," the neighbor said. "Chummy is playing in the snow in your yard right now."

My niece, thinking her mother and I had planned to surprise her, called her three boys, Lee, Lynn, and Leslie, and rushed to the door to greet us. There they saw Chum cavorting in the snow, rolling in it, making his tunnels and throwing it over his back.

My niece called, "Come here, Chummy, you're all wet!"

He stopped playing and looked at her, happily prancing on his hind feet. The boys saw that he had no intention of coming in and started out to catch him—and he simply disappeared before their very eyes. So positive were they that it really was Chum, they made a thorough search of the neighborhood but without success. Something told Patty they had seen an apparition and she hastened to telephone her mother in the Florida hospital.

My sister surmised at once that Chummy was dead and had gone north for a last play in the snow he loved and to say goodbye to the rest of the family.

And I knew he had appeared in Rochester (where so far as I know, he was the only black Pomeranian) to prove to me that he simply had gone on ahead to wait for me.

—*Alicia Mason, Miami Beach, Fla.*

The Friendship

We had two cats a couple of years ago—Jordan, a big orange fellow with golden eyes and a warm friendly heart. He was the only orange cat in our neighborhood and a great treasure to us. The other was a little black cat who came along and we took him in. The children named him Glenn (for a movie star) because of his sleek maleness. Jordan adopted him at once and the little one responded in kind, following the big cat everywhere and always lying near him on the couch. They sometimes tumbled and wrestled, or raced across the front lawn nipping at each other, but always affectionately.

The night of May 11, 1965, my daughter Martha Jane came in late from her college library. She was crying bitterly and holding the limp body of big Jordan in her arms. She had found him in the street, evidently hit by a car.

We missed him very much but had to resign ourselves to the loss of the affectionate little creature. Glenn wasn't so adaptable, however. For the next two days he prowled in and out of the house anxiously searching for his old friend and incidentally keeping alive our grief—but there was nothing we could do.

Then death struck again. This time May 13, 1965, I found the small black heap in front of our house. In his inexperience and loneliness, Glenn had wandered into the street and a speeding car had hit him. My husband buried him in the backyard. Ours was a depressed household.

Two nights later, Martha Jane was returning from class with a student friend. She told him on the way home about our cat disasters. He was interested and sympathetic but as his car turned onto our street and his headlights swept our lawn, he exclaimed, "Well, what are you talking about? Aren't those two cats the ones you just described to me?"

My daughter looked over the lawn, garishly green in the bright lights, and saw a large orange cat gracefully leap across the grass while running alongside a small black friend playfully nipped at his flanks. She called to them through the open car window but they ran past her, through the hedges and into the black night.

No one ever has seen them again, but we don't grieve for them anymore.

—*Martha Adams, Oakland, Calif.*

Death's Black Harbinger

Twice in my life the death of someone I dearly loved has been preceded by a visit of what I have come to call the black bird of death.

The first time, I was a child of 12 living with my mother in Claymont, Delaware. I had no brothers or sisters, but I never was lonely for Mother spent long hours reading to me and talking about my father who died in my infancy. When she spoke of my father, her far-off look frightened me. I felt she wished to go to him. Often at such times she would take to her bed and become so ill that a nurse had to come in to care for her.

During one of her illnesses in the summer of 1950, I first saw the ominous bird. The nurse told me Mother was too ill to see me and I could find nothing to do but go to bed at dusk. I quickly fell asleep and darkness had not yet come when a shrill cry awakened me. From my bed, I saw a great black bird perched atop my dresser, its silky feathers shining in the fading glow of twilight. The high-held head was large and round and above a narrow beak two emerald eyes glared down at me.

Suddenly its wings spread and flapped violently; fierce cries came from its throat. I lay terrified, unable to understand this monstrosity. Finally sheer horror impelled me to jump from bed and lift the window screen so the bird could get out. I don't know how it entered; all the windows in the house were screened.

I ran to tell the nurse of my frightening experience and met her coming from my mother's room. She told me my mother had just died, and the strange bird suddenly lost its importance.

I mourned my mother and missed her terribly, but I believed she had gone to my father as she had longed to do. I was taken in by Aunt Sarah, my mother's younger sister, who lived in nearby Wilmington. Aunt Sarah, married but childless, was like my mother in many ways— a warm, gentle, lovely woman—but she was strong and healthy, as my mother never had been. Aunt Sarah's seaman husband seldom was at home, and she spent most of her time with me as my mother had done. In the next five years, I grew to love her dearly.

Then in January 1955, when I was 17, again I found the black bird in my bedroom. This time I couldn't see it clearly, for it was midnight and very dark. Its emerald eyes penetrated the darkness, glaring into mine, and its cries chilled me to the marrow. Again it left when I opened the window.

In the morning I found my Aunt Sarah dead.

—*Clara McCue, Chester, Pa.*

Never a Sparrow Falls

The lenten days were bleak in Kansas City, Missouri, in 1956 and the cloister of the monastery of the Augustinian Fathers damp and subdued as Holy Week approached. I had been working a long time on a mural there and on Good Friday I would be finished.

Ash Wednesday I reached home late and over coffee I sketched various designs for one section of the mural, which did not quite satisfy me. Suddenly, I was astonished to see that I had written a sentence.

"Tell David to let the cat out." At the same time I heard the gravelly voice of David Imboden's wife Hazel saying "He'll know what I mean ..."

Hazel had died in August 1955, and her studio behind the main house had been closed, but so certain was I that I had heard her voice, I wrote a note to her husband and immediately ran down to mail it.

On Good Friday, I finished the mural and found a note from David pinned to my screen door when I returned to my studio. "Must see you right away." I fully expected an inquisition and derision.

Not so. He told me that when he opened the door to Hazel's studio the strong and unmistakable odor of cat almost knocked him over. Next he saw a streak of darkness as the cat itself whizzed past him.

Now he could stop grieving for Hazel. My scribbled sentence, itself a deep enough mystery to us, was even more confusing, for Hazel had no cat. Apparently the animal had slipped into the apartment at the time Hazel had been taken to the hospital. David had no reason for going into the studio after she died until her sympathy for the cat reached out through the veil to give me the message.

Yes, we survive. Cats, too. I believe it unswervingly since that Good Friday in 1956. And I am reassured that never a sparrow falls but a hand reaches out to catch it.

—*Joseph Heidt,*
Snowmass, Colo.

Ghost Encounters of Children and Encounters with Children's Ghosts

Kids see ghosts all the time—until we train them not to. "It's just your imagination." The ghost of Grandpa must just wink when he hears that. He knows better. And so does little Suzy. And what if what we call "imagination" is more real than what we call "reality?" Seeing into the spirit world seems to be a natural human ability that we all have—until it is conditioned out of us. How can we concentrate on making a killing in the stock market if there are spooks flitting about all the time?

From the other side of the phenomenon, children often appear as ghosts, and the voices of children are very frequently recorded in experiments with electronic voice phenomena (EVP). Many of these may be the spirits of departed children, but others may be the spirits of adults who have regressed to their childhood after death. And still others may be childish inhabitants of the spirit world who have never had a material existence—adolescent fairies, perhaps.

The Friendly Spook

In June 1955, my son Jared attended Presidio Junior High School in San Francisco, California. Jared always had been a good student, but algebra was not his forte. He was very worried the day before his final examination in algebra.

He said, "This test counts for one-third of my grade for the semester. If I don't get a good grade, I will not be able to graduate from school this term."

I told him I would pray for him, but he must overcome his fear of the exam. I said fear was faith in failure and that he needed to have faith in success.

The night before the exam, he studied diligently and I prayed with fervor that he would pass the test. The next day, he left for school confident he would make a good grade in the examination. He had finished about two-thirds of the test before he was stymied.

Just then, a boy his own age who was a complete stranger to him bent over Jared's desk and told him how to work the rest of the equations. When the time limit for the test had elapsed, Jared went to the teacher to ask him why he had permitted this other boy to help him. Jared explained that the other boy didn't give away any answers, but merely told how to solve the problems.

The teacher said he didn't realize anyone had given Jared any help. Jared then described the appearance of the boy.

His teacher looked at him with amazement and said, "That description fits John, a former student of mine who burned to death in this building eight years ago! He was one of my best students."

—Betty Middlebrook, San Francisco, Calif.

The Phantom Baby

The planting season was at its peak when my mother and father moved into the old house in Grayson, Kentucky, in 1911. I wasn't born yet but my eldest sister was almost two and, like most children at that age, demanded almost constant care. Since Dad was busy getting the seed into the ground, Mom was left alone for many hours with only the baby.

It was on just such a lonely spring day, Mom says, that she first heard the haunting sounds that were to drive the family from the old country house, abandoning the crops Dad had planted so laboriously.

Mom had put the baby to sleep and then hurried to the yard to gather wood chips to start the dinner fire in the old coal cook-stove. She barely had begun when from the house came the frail, pitiful wail of a baby, sounding more like the cry of a newborn child than of one nearly two. Mom dropped the chips and rushed into the house, only to find her baby still sleeping peacefully.

But the crying persisted. Mom searched from the first floor to the attic, but found nothing.

The wailing continued on and off for the next three weeks until Mom was reaching the point of a nervous breakdown. There was nothing to do but move.

A week before they left the old house, Mom learned the sad story that explained the phantom baby.

A neighbor told her that several years before, a young unwed girl gave birth to a baby in one of the upstairs bedrooms. Trying desperately to conceal this fact from the girl's father, she and her mother pretended she needed a cough remedy. The mother sent her husband to a neighboring farm.

Meanwhile, the baby was delivered but the girl's mother was so afraid her husband would return too soon that she wrapped the infant in a blanket and stuffed it in a dresser drawer. There the baby suffocated.

At the first opportunity, the body was removed to the garden and secretly buried beneath some shrubs in a shallow grave. And so the legend of the phantom baby whose cries haunt the old house. No one has been able to live there since.

—*Juanita Johnson, Flatwoods, Ky.*

We Saw Not

All of our six children had invisible playmates, the Little People, and animals, too, like the white horse from Castle-Onee. We grown-ups related to these invisibles rather casually, not thinking that this psychic faculty of the children could be the means of strengthening our belief in the survival of the personality after death.

My oldest brother, Buster Orr, had died of a bullet wound at the age of 21 far from home. Four months after his death, my sister Phyllis, our two younger brothers, Jack and Maurice, and I, with our families, all were at Mother's house on Report Street in Stockton, California, for dinner. During the course of the meal, Lucy, my three-year-old, suddenly asked, "Why does Buster always come to the table but never eat?"

A hushed silence came over all of us... as each of us felt truly that Buster was there with us and wanted us to know through this little child that he was back home and all right.

Lucy has a family of her own now. But I have remained grateful through the years for the message she gave us when: Having eyes we saw not.

—*Hazel Orr Coffey, Monteca, Calif.*

Grandpa's Ghost

My maternal grandfather, the Honorable George Washington Rose, an attorney, was accidently shot and killed by his oldest son, my Uncle Oliver Steele, then 22 years old, in 1880. At that time my mother, the youngest of a family of four children, was seven.

From then on, the 16-room mansion in which the family lived in Maysville, Missouri, had the reputation of being haunted by Grandpa's ghost. Many times he was heard walking about the place and at other times was seen by various members of the family.

One evening when I was 10 years old and living with my parents in the country, about three miles southeast of Maysville, I suddenly became violently ill with what later was diagnosed as "bilious fever." My mother, seeing my distress, tried to interest me in playing dominoes to distract me from my sickness. But I started vomiting, violently.

We didn't have any telephone and my mother, becoming alarmed, started walking with me to the nearest neighbors, about a quarter of a mile away up a steep hill. She wished to telephone my father, who was working away from home and was with us only on weekends. She wished to call a doctor also. I vomited all the way up the hill, along the dusty road.

When we reached the top of the hill, I looked back down at our house in the valley; it was bathed in evening sunshine.

In a triangular clearing between the house, the smokehouse, and a woodpile, I saw three men. They were dressed in black; their frock coats and tall stovepipe hats, which long since had gone out of fashion, were clearly visible in the brilliant sunshine. Even from a quarter of a mile away, I could see these men distinctly. They were milling around in the clearing in our back yard.

"There's Pa!" I heard my mother gasp. "Down there. Look!"

I looked at her and saw that her eyes were focused on the same distant scene.

"It's Pa and two of his associates," she exclaimed.

I've never forgotten that long-ago vision and I've often wondered at the cause of it. Was it because I was indeed near death and almost "over on the other side" that I saw these men? Or was it simply that my mother, a reputed psychic and medium, transferred this scene from her mind to mine? Specifically, were the men actually there or simply in our minds? The fact that we both saw this scene must have some significance.

—Cecile Ward, Chicago, Ill.

The Nonbeliever

When I was a small child, I knew my sister Dollie was something of a mystic. She often foretold things that later happened just the way she said—which surprised friends and family.

It happened that my grandfather and Dollie, who was only 15, died at my father's house on the same night—January 31, 1906. My grandfather's trouble was mostly old age; my sister had typhoid fever and complications. Because she was SO young, her death was tragic. She was the favorite of the other seven children and the whole family was broken-hearted.

My mother had been raised to believe in spiritual things and always thought there were ghosts and a chance of our departed ones getting in touch with us, one way or another. My father really was vexed by her views and ridiculed her. He said there was no such thing as a ghost and if he saw anything mysterious, he would shoot through it.

We were poor country farmers and in need of many things, so when my father heard of a job in a western state, he went there to work for a few months. On his return home, there was a distance of 25 miles from the railroad station for which he had no conveyance, so he decided to walk.

During the night, he was so sleepy he had to stop and sleep awhile by the side of the road. He found a flat rock for his head and was preparing to rest when my dead sister suddenly appeared near him. He spoke her name and asked her what she wanted. He reached for her, but she vanished. He told us his first thought was to take her home, and he stayed there for some time hoping she would reappear, but he did not see her again.

Here is something we often wondered about: Dollie was dressed not in the white dress she was buried in, but in a white blouse and black skirt and cap—the style in those days. The clothes Father saw her wearing were at home in a trunk.

My mother always said Dollie appeared to show my father that the spirit lives after death.

—E. S., Hutchinson, Kans.

My Ghostly Customers

In the summer of 1930, I worked as a waitress at Nelson's Creamery in Glendale, California. Nelson's was a small cafe with eight stools near the front and a butter and egg sales counter in the rear.

I was cleaning the shelves beneath the rear counter one afternoon when Rose, the other waitress, went into the back room to get a can of buttermilk. No one was in the store, but I kept an eye on the front door, the only entrance and exit for customers. Once when I glanced at the counter, I saw an elderly woman standing behind a stool. Smiling, she placed an old-fashioned Concord grape basket on the counter. She was dressed in the "Gay Nineties" style and I thought she must be a movie extra doing some between-the-scenes shopping until I realized no one was making a movie right then in Glendale.

When Rose stepped back into the room I asked her to wait on the woman because my uniform was unsightly from the dusty shelves. Rose glanced around the room, brushed right past the old lady and then said, "I don't see anyone."

The old lady merely smiled and nodded.

"Over here, Rose," I said and turned to apologize to the customer. She had disappeared! I was the only one to see her. I quit trying to convince Rose when she began giving me strange looks.

Two weeks later, a little girl who looked to be about six years old skipped past two men sitting at the counter. Stepping over to the egg counter, she lifted the corners of her pinafore, curtsied, and smiled at me.

I finished pouring coffee for my other customers and turned to the little girl. She was gone.

I asked the men seated at the counter whether she had gone out. Looking quite perplexed, they shook their heads—and my mind skipped back to the old lady with the grape basket.

"Nobody came in," one of the men said.

"She did too," I insisted, "a little girl wearing a pink-and-white checked dress and a white pinafore. And her hair was in long curls."

"You're tired," one man said. "Why don't you quit?"

I did—that night. Waitress work is hard enough without having to deal with spirit customers.

—Mae Gettel,
Redwood Estates, Calif.

Phantom Vehicles and Buildings

There was once a time in America when traveling carnivals and fairs would highlight their midway attractions with the viewings of certain famous "death cars." And while no one may have seen the ghost of James Dean at the county fair behind the 4–H building, ghost cars, ghost trains, and all manner of vehicle have been reported by numerous *FATE* readers since the magazine's inception in 1948. And before that, the mariner terror the Flying Dutchmen vexed sailors and landlubbers alike with tales spectral encounters upon the high seas. So it's no wonder that reports of places that seem to be out of sync with time continue to be reported.

The highways of North America have created tales of phantom cars that appear out of nowhere and help stranded motorists who later discover they were aided by the dead. And old tales of spectral ships helmed by doomed crews still inspire the imagination as well as turn the stomach at the thought of such a tormented existence.

But make no mistake; whether you travel by land, sea, or air, you always have the chance of encountering travelers who might not exist on the same plane as you and me. Let the following chapter act as your guide in what to expect should a phantom vehicle or house interrupt your journey through life.

The House that Didn't Change

In 1910 my father built a bungalow in Lemoore, California, a town in the center of the San Joaquin Valley. It was square with a lean-to kitchen in back and a pyramid-shaped roof. The house was painted yellow and the roof green. Near the back porch, my father dug a well with a green hand-pump, which poured into a homemade wooden sink. On the front porch was a rocker of bent willow branches covered with a cushion and matching back pad, which my mother made of a lovely flowered material.

How well I remember the details of that house located on the dusty lane called Magnolia Avenue, although the trees that lined both sides were small, young cottonwoods. Each day I traveled along the lane on my way to and from school, making sure to keep way over to the side to avoid the thick dust. I passed several houses then crossed the heavy wooden bridge over the irrigation canal. After I passed the high red livery stable, I turned along the paved street to school.

My father never did have time to plant grass or shrubs in the front yard, for he was taken ill with typhoid fever as soon as he finished the house. Soon it was discovered that the well water had been poisoned by seepage and had caused his illness, so the well was condemned. The pump was taken off and the pipe capped.

We moved after two years, taking all the furniture, including the willow rocker.

I did not return to the town of my childhood until 1942. Some towns do not change much, and this one certainly hadn't, except for automobiles instead of buggies and service stations scattered here and there. Having some time to myself, I decided to see how Magnolia Avenue looked after 30 years. I had heard all the streets in that section of town had been paved, and I prepared myself for any other changes that might have occurred. If the house was still there, I thought, it probably would look very old.

As I came to the intersection, I was startled to see the old livery stable still standing on the corner. And when I crossed the street and stood at the entrance to Magnolia Avenue, I found myself looking down the same dusty lane it had been in 1910. I crossed the old wooden bridge and, keeping to the side of the lane, avoided the thick dust that was still there. As I passed under the cottonwoods, I noticed they hadn't grown at all.

When I came to the bungalow with the pyramid roof, I certainly was not prepared for what I saw. Standing right in front of me was a new house with a green roof and yellow walls. It looked exactly the same! Not even the shingles were curled, cracked, or rotted. And on the front porch was a willow rocker with matching cushions and back pad in the same flowered pattern! I looked past the yard, still wild with weeds, and saw a green pump on the side porch over a homemade wooden sink.

And although it looked as if it had not been touched since we moved, the house did not look vacant. The front door was open and I stood in front trying to see if there was someone inside. Since I could see no one, I thought I would go to the door and knock, but every time I tried to step into the yard, my legs suddenly seemed too heavy to move.

I walked up and down in front, still hoping to see someone, until I noticed there wasn't even a soul on the street. Although it was 1:00 p.m. on a bright, balmy day, there were no sounds, no birds, no people, nothing. I began to feel uneasy, fearing that if someone came out of the door, it would be my dead parents. I turned to leave, knowing it would be wrong to defy the barrier, to enter the house.

I went back up the dusty lane, under the cottonwoods, over the wooden bridge, past the livery stable, and away. I have never returned.

—*Dulcie Brown, Fresno, Calif.*

I Rode a Death Car

I felt a chill run down my back when I awoke in my dimly lit room on November 4, 1951, in Superior, Wisconsin. Looking at the clock, I saw that it was too early to get up on a Sunday morning, so I climbed back into bed.

The next thing I remember is being in a car that was racing wildly through the dawn. I felt an unspeakable terror as I reared back, instinctively pushed my feet hard against the floorboard, and, at the same time, tried to grab the steering wheel.

I became more frightened when I saw my reckless driver's face. He was very dark. I tried to scream when suddenly I saw a large obstruction looming directly ahead of us. I clawed frantically at the man's arm. He was staring straight ahead, his arms rigid. He tried to speak—and in that instant we crashed. I could not feel nor hear a thing, but I began fighting desperately to push a thin, wet vapor-like substance from my eyes and mouth.

Suddenly, I was back in bed, in my room.

I got up and tried to dress, but I was trembling so that I couldn't manage it for a few moments. I ran my hands unbelievingly down my gown, which was soaked, and through my clinging, wet hair.

"Oh, what a horrible, horrible nightmare!" I cried to myself.

I finished dressing and hurried to catch the Duluth-Superior bus I always rode to church. Although I waited a long time, the bus didn't come. I was about to give up and go home when a passerby told me there had been a serious accident on the interstate bridge, delaying traffic (and my bus) until the bridge could be repaired.

The next day, the Superior Evening Telegram carried a story that an Indian named Ernest Cloud had crashed his car at high speed into the Duluth-Superior bridge, which connected the two cities. The Indian was drowned in the deep waters of the bay. Apparently Ernest Cloud had been drinking.

I still feel that I was a passenger in that death car hurtling toward a watery grave. I never heard of this man before I read about him in the Telegram and I wonder why I was chosen for this terrifying experience.

The public library in Superior, Wisconsin, contains microfilm files of Ernest Cloud's death as reported in the November 5, 1951, issue of the Superior Evening Telegram.

—*Hazel Welch, Superior, Wis.*

Vanishing Car

I was raised in Florida back in the days when the roads were of brick and just nine feet wide. There were stretches where no buildings could be seen for miles, just swamp and timberland.

One night in 1934, my family and I were driving on such a stretch of road between Bartow and Ft. Meade, following the taillight of another car. There were six of us in our Studebaker, and I was sitting in the front seat. The car in front of us was a Model T Ford and we could see plainly its shape and its passengers.

We followed this car a long distance, because to pass we would have to run off the road into some deep sand holes. Suddenly, right in front of all six of us, the car we were following just moved sideways off the road and into the swamp.

My father jammed on the brakes. We could not understand what happened. The car had not driven off the road, but just had drifted sideways. We pointed our headlights into the swamp and we looked with flashlights, but we could find no sign of that car.

We had followed it for about 40 miles, down narrow road and around sharp corners. It was a clear night. How could this other car just vanish?

Needless to say, when we resumed our journey we felt quite shaken.

—*Lois B. Tracy, Wise, Va.*

Phantom Travelers

Recently my friend Harriette Huson, who lives in Buena Park, California, some 20 miles from my home, called to tell me of a strange and frightening experience she had had the night before while on her way home from visiting me.

Harriette said she was driving about 50 miles an hour on a two-lane highway in heavy traffic, with the oncoming lane just a little better, when suddenly an old truck slowly pulled across her path. She was so sure of a collision that she braced herself even as she pulled as far right as she dared, hoping to avoid the truck.

She said, "I couldn't have missed it—as close as it was! I looked in my rearview mirror after I was past and a modern car was close behind. The truck couldn't have wedged into the line of cars. That means I had to go through it!"

I told her that I believed she had driven through the truck and that my husband and I had had a similar experience in 1929 on a narrow road between Tulsa and Sapulpa, Oklahoma.

We had visited my husband's parents in Sapulpa and were on our way home to Tulsa. We were driving a Model T Ford roadster and doing a pretty good clip for that time and that car. I held my 18-month-old son on my lap. We weren't talking and the baby was asleep. Car lights were not what they are today, and we drove almost dead center on that narrow road for we couldn't see very far ahead. No cars were behind or in front of us.

Then suddenly, right in front of the car, a covered wagon lumbered!

I gasped and my husband instantly swerved the car far to the left since there seemed to be the most room on that side. We bumped to a halt on the grassy shoulder of the road.

We jumped out of the car to find that we were the only living things in sight. All was silence. There was no wagon. There was nothing.

I think we yelped in unison: "That was a covered wagon!"

Both talking at once, we tried to describe what we had seen. Each of us had seen a barrel inside the wagon, the food box on the back, and a frying pan and tub hanging from the food box. But it wasn't there! We had nearly collided with a covered wagon that wasn't there!

Perhaps one might say that Harriette was miraculously saved from falling asleep at the wheel when the phantom truck crossed her path. Or that it was a dream. But I am sure the truck was there to see, but not to touch or hit.

—*Thelma Gibson Young, Pomona, Calif.*

New Haven's Phantom Ship of 1646

Every Connecticut history book contains the story of the strange incidents surrounding the loss, reappearance, and final disappearance of "the great ship" of New Haven, Connecticut. There are many records still in existence today which attest to the authenticity of this incredible tale.

Cotton Mather wrote of the story in *Magnalia Christi Americana* (London, 1702) explaining that he had the story in a personal letter from The Rev. James Pierpont. The 1893 editor of the poems of Henry Wadsworth Longfellow (New York, Nathan Dole, editor) told the story of New Haven's ghost ship in a series of quatrains. More formal historical evidence for the authenticity of the story appears in the official records of the New Haven Colony and the New Haven Historical Society. Besides their official records, the library of the Historical Society contains no less than six books which relate the story of "the great ship": Charles M. Andrews' *The Colonial Period of American History*, Edward Atwater's *History of the Colony of New Haven*, Alexander Johnston's *Connecticut: A Study of a Commonwealth Democracy*, James Savage's *Winthrop's History of New England*, Thomas J. Wetenbaker's *The First Americans, 1607–1690*, and Rollin G. Osterweis' *Three Centuries of New Haven*.

Shortly after their arrival to the south central Connecticut port city in 1638, the early inhabitants set about establishing profitable trade relations with both the Southern Colonies and with the West Indies. Unfortunately, however, political problems—especially attacks by Dutch and Swedish forces—soon cut deeply into their trading expeditions and these financial losses were felt keenly in New Haven.

Finally, in an all-out effort to rebuild a successful trade, recoup their numerous financial losses, and save the colony, the leading men of the town formed a company, purchased a large ship known as the Fellowship and prepared to send it to England loaded with trade items lumber, hides, peas, and wheat.

"The Company of Merchants of New Haven" was formed in 1645 amid the good wishes of the colonists—most of whom had invested in it and eagerly looked forward to its success.

The old sailors among the settlers disliked the looks of the Fellowship—even its new captain, George Lamberton, admitted it seemed somewhat "cranky." But the trip had been decided upon, and everyone in the colony donated something to the community cargo. The passenger list included some of the colony's most important citizens, Nathaniel Turner, captain of the military company; Mrs. Stephen Goodyear, wife of the colony's wealthiest citizen; and Thomas Gregson, a civic and religious leader.

The Fellowship sailed for England in January 1646.

Almost the entire colony watched the ship break through the ice of the harbor, sail into Long Island Sound and on out into the Atlantic as it began the long trip to England. The following winter was a lonely one, and everyone's thoughts were on the Fellowship with which their hopes and many of their loved ones were crossing the sea.

Summer came at long last and with the warmer weather came the arrival of numerous English ships. But there was no word of the Fellowship.

Nevertheless, the colonists' spirits remained unflagging. "After all," said the English sailors, "ships are often blown off their courses at sea and are delayed for many weeks."

But summer dragged into fall and there was still no word. Winter came again and with its coming hope gave way. Many families donned mourning robes and publicly grieved for their lost families.

By New Year's Day 1648, two years after the ship set sail, all hope was long gone.

One afternoon during the following June 1648, when the Fellowship had been given up by all, a thunderstorm hit New Haven Colony. However, the men and women continued to go about their business. Then—an hour before sunset—someone glanced toward the harbor and there was the Fellowship! Immediately, crowds gathered on the shore and many of the colonists wept openly at the sight.

There it was—"the great ship!" On its deck, Captain Lamberton could be seen proudly standing. Although clouds seemed to surround the vessel as it moved closer to the shore, it was nonetheless clearly visible to everyone.

But suddenly there came a change. A wind sprang up and the ship's topmasts began to blow off. In minutes they were hanging, tangled in the rigging. Then all the masts began to fall overboard; the hull capsized and a huge cloud enveloped the ship.

Then there was nothing! The clouds lifted. The winds became calm. The Fellowship had disappeared.

No trace was ever found, no news was ever heard of "the great ship." On that June evening in 1648, the men and women of New Haven Colony walked from the shore stunned.

A churchman tried to comfort them, explaining that God had sent them this sign to show them how their loved ones and their ship had been lost at sea.

Of course "all things are possible," but how wonderful it would be if we could understand exactly how the "mechanics" of our world operate to make a vision such as this possible. Three hundred and twenty-two years have passed since the New Haven colonists watched a ship that wasn't there, saw it sink in a place where its sinking did not occur, and we know no more about the energies which govern these "odd" occurrences than they did.

—*William Rutledge III*

Spirits of the Railroads

Common knowledge, coupled with the sage advice of our elders, has led us to rest secure in the knowledge that "there is no such thing as a ghost," and that it is childish for an adult to believe in—much less write about them.

But millions of people around the world have seen the shades of the departed, both human and animal, and no society on the planet has a dearth of lore on the subject of dealing with ghosts when they appear to us: How do we appease them, how do we banish them (if necessary) or simply, how do we honor the dead and assure their peace?

In the industrial world, it is not uncommon to learn of cases in which the living have encountered ghostly images. These include nonliving things, such as ethereal houses, automobiles, and in some rare instances, entire ghost villages which, like Brigadoon, are not there the following morning. Therefore, the case involving a phantom locomotive should not cause us to raise our eyebrows. Or should it?

After the completion of the coast-to-coast railway system at the end of the 19th century, the United States boasted one of the busiest rail systems in the world. Enormous trains like the Mikado hauled vast numbers of coal cars to feed the industrial appetite of the budding world superpower. Pittsburgh, in particular, needed coal to fuel the blast furnaces of its titanic steel, glass, and iron works, and was serviced by a number of crisscrossing railways.

Phantom Locomotive

The building of the interstate highway network, the decline of commerce by rail, and the advent of the postmodern era led to the obsolescence and eventual abandonment of the railways and of the tunnels that were blasted through the heart of the Appalachians.

One such train track ran through tunnels south of Pittsburgh, near the city of Canonsburg. It retains a ghostly memory of its heyday, as two young Pennsylvanians were able to discover for themselves.

While driving along the back roads running off Donaldson Road, they came upon long-abandoned rails, rusted and interspersed with weeds. A pair of tunnels farther down the line caught their attention—particularly the fact that one of the tubes was barricaded by a gate that swung aside as they approached, as if beckoning to them.

Discretion prevailing over valor, they chose to forgo the dubious distinction of venturing into the darkened tunnel's nether reality. They decided to return during the day, only to discover, in the best horror-film fashion, that the gates were no longer there. In their place now stood a wall of old bricks, the work of earlier decades, judging from their poor condition. This disconcerted the youths even further.

Unable to ignore the site's enigmatic attraction, they returned to the tunnels one night during a full moon in May 1993. Any plans they may have entertained about exploring the abandoned tunnels were thwarted by the sudden appearance of a phantom locomotive, pearly white in color and almost solid, which caused them to lose their resolve and run away.

Massive Train Wreck

They bestowed the name "Hell" upon the peculiar patch of backwoods they had discovered, and began to learn as much about it as they could. A quick check at their local library revealed nothing, at first. But they gradually pieced together the story of a massive train wreck, with considerable loss of life that had taken place along that section of track in the 1930s.

Even more ominous, their research uncovered the story of a subsequent derailment during the late 1960s along the same section of track. This caused a collision with a train carrying the bodies of Vietnam War veterans.

"Hell" had a personality of its own, as they discovered. It allowed some to enter its unhallowed confines while chasing others away, availing itself of a bright yellow Chevy Camaro or an equally garish pickup truck that would pursue unwelcome arrivals back to the main road, then turn aside down a dirt track just as soon as the trespassers had been warned off.

Before discarding the teenagers' narrative as a lively amalgam of Freddy Krueger films and Stephen King novels, we should reflect upon the fact that acts of violence tend to leave an indelible imprint upon the areas in which they occur.

The late British psychic, John Pendragon, reported an event that took place in London during World War II. While seeking shelter in a bombed-out mansion during an air raid, a man came upon a "monster," which he described as being horned, goat-like, and filled with evil, sitting on the stairs leading to the upper floor. The nightmarish beast ran up the stairs, the man claimed, and vanished into one of the bedrooms, where it proceeded to make loud noises.

Pendragon speculated that the hapless man had witnessed an elemental, a creature "prone to frequent places where a tragedy has occurred." Subsequent investigation revealed that a manservant had committed suicide on the premises by hanging himself from a banister, and many people had since reported the horned, bestial apparition on the steps. Enigmatic three-toed footprints were found in the vicinity of Mars, Pennsylvania, in February 1975, at the site of a railroad tunnel that had collapsed, a fact that lends some weight to the tragic event suggestion.

The Canonsburg, Pennsylvania, region falls loosely under the general zone known as the Laurel Highlands. This area is well known for its UFO and Bigfoot sightings. Other railroad mysteries in the region oddly complement the teens' story. During the completion of the track leading down from Pennview Mountain, two gangs of railroad workers, sparked either by the hot summer weather or a real or imaginary slight, stopped driving spikes into the ground and instead, chose to drive them into one another. By the time the situation was resolved, two men lay dead and were promptly buried on the site.

According to locals, on certain evenings voices arguing in rage can be heard.

A parallel situation to the Canonsburg sighting was recorded in the book *Illustrated Guide to Ghosts* by Nancy

Roberts. Pat Hayes and her husband Larry were driving through North Carolina in the early morning hours when their car broke down. While Larry was getting help, Pat heard a screech of metal in the darkness. She got out of the vehicle to see what was happening.

She soon witnessed the derailment of a passenger train from a tall bridge into the waters of a creek below. Explosions, fire, and screams rent the darkness. To add to her bewilderment, she found herself standing beside a thin, uniformed man who asked her for the time, yet seemed unconcerned by the calamitous situation playing out before them.

Her husband returned to find her distraught, convinced that there had been a terrible accident in the woods.

The following day, they visited the local train station, where they learned that there had been no derailment that evening—but there had been one on that very same evening exactly 50 years before. On August 27, 1891, a train had left Sallsbury for Ashboro, North Carolina, and reached Bostian's Bridge at 3 a.m., plunging 90 feet into the dark water below.

The stationmaster was even able to show the confused and frightened Mrs. Hayes a clip from the *Charlotte Chronicle* that memorialized the terrible event: "Hurled to death, 30 Killed, Many Injured. At Three O'Clock in the Morning, Bridge near Statesville the Scene of the Wreck."

Baggage master H. K. Linster was killed in the disaster. His description matched that of the man she'd spoken to at the crash site.

Even more dramatic are accounts of the "headless track walker" who carries out his duty at night to this very day.

As one variant of the story has it, the track walker was on his way back to Derry, Pennsylvania, after checking certain sections of track in the vicinity of Burd's Crossing, when he was slain by a westbound train. The fact of the matter is that the unnamed man's headless corpse was found on the tracks the next day. Ever since, those taking shortcuts across the track have stumbled across the path of a headless man carrying a lantern before him.

While we should not allow the charm of folklore, no matter how colorful, to distract us from the underlying truth of the matter at hand, places like "Hell" exist not only in the U.S., but around the world, many of them involve railroads.

—*Scott Corrales, FATE contributing writer*

Dead Zones

These so-called "Dead Zones" have increasingly attracted the attention of researchers bent on unlocking their secrets. Their existence has been explained in terms of "psychic saturation," a concept that presumes matter is quite capable of recording impressions of diverse natures, much like a blank strip of magnetic tape.

When an event produces an intense outburst of mental or spiritual power from an individual or a group of persons, surrounding matter (the tunnels, train tracks, etc., in this case) picks up the outburst, storing it for "playback" (for want of a better term) by a person or persons capable of doing so.

While neither of the two percipients of the strange phenomena taking place at "Hell" tried to test the solidity of the gate at the tunnel entrance or that of the phantom locomotive, the phenomenon has entered playback mode whenever they have returned.

An alternative theory, that of psychic contagion, could be invoked to explain the goings-on in this community near a major interstate highway (Route 79), less than 40 minutes from Pittsburgh.

The events playing out at "Hell" are nothing more than a hallucination suffered by someone at a particular time—perhaps during the collision in the 1930s, or during the derailment of the 1960s that has repeated itself and expanded until it developed into a sort of localized mental disturbance, infecting those entering the area and spread by them to others, fueling the phenomenon's existence.

While such situations have been discussed by eminent American and European parapsychologists, their complexity leads one to choose the possibility of a bona fide haunting.

In all fairness, one must point out that other train accidents have occurred in Pennsylvania and have left no haunting tales for posterity.

In 1856, a train filled with Sunday school children on an excursion crashed to a regular train, leaving 66 dead. The engineer was reportedly so distraught that he committed suicide on returning home.

In 1943, a wheel bearing froze on the seventh car of the Congressional Limited as it sped through Philadelphia. The train ground to a halt and the seventh car jumped the track, slamming into the embankment. Other cars left the rails and piled up, causing 79 deaths.

There may be no quick and easy answer to explain the situation. Pennsylvania is filled with ghost stories and mysterious areas, which add to the Keystone State's store of the rare and unusual. The phantom trains are just one example.

Bigfoot and Train Wreck Haunt the Same Area

Interestingly enough, there is researched Bigfoot activity in the area connected with the Canonsburg ghost train. Devon Ross and John Stasko, investigators for the Pennsylvania Association for the Study of the Unexplained, visited the area in September 1991 with the intention of conducting a "Bigfoot Stake-out." Their area of study, coincidentally, was the backyard of a house located on the same section of railroad track that the local teenagers would come to identify as "Hell" two years later.

Armed with flashlights and communicating with each other through radio headsets, the investigators' efforts were rewarded by the sight of two pairs of green eyes staring back at them in the darkness. At nearly 11 o'clock at night, there was a sound of heavy footfalls crashing through the woods, followed by the sound of metallic ringing against the rails.

It was then that two figures, described as "flat black and with arms swinging wildly," ran across their line of sight, never looking back at the investigators. The creatures were described as being between five and six feet tall, and weighing some 150 pounds. The erratic mariner in which they moved has also been reported in other cases involving Bigfoot-like creatures.

—*Keith Bastianini, FATE contributing writer*

Saved from Disaster by a Phantom Auto

It still seems incredible, but one of the strangest incidents of my life occurred 45 years ago when I first started driving.

It all began on a bright sunny day in the fall of 1949 as I raced along the highways of Ohio. I was happy with my new job. I was delivering dentures and eyeglasses to out-of-town doctors from the Cleveland Laboratories. I had the full-time use of a late model company car.

As I approached Cleveland from the west side, everything seemed normal. The 1947 Studebaker I drove handled very nicely as I proceeded east on Lake Avenue. I had made several green lights, and only one more traffic signal remained before hitting the fast expressway that would zip me nonstop to downtown Cleveland.

As I approached the intersection, the traffic signal turned yellow and I applied more pressure to the accelerator to beat the light. My car jumped ahead, and I just barely cleared the intersection as the light turned red.

It was a short distance to the next corner where a black 1937 sedan pulled out in front of me traveling very slowly. I hit my brake to slow down and to my dismay discovered that the brakes didn't work. I applied my brake pedal over and over again, but to no avail.

The situation became more drastic as the black sedan came to a complete halt at the very next corner. It was trying to make a turn and was waiting for the oncoming traffic to clear. I became frantic as I closed within a few feet of the sedan and saw a woman and a young girl sitting in front.

I honked my horn to warn them, but they ignored me. I couldn't veer to the left because of the oncoming traffic, and I couldn't veer to the right because of the parked cars along the curb. There wasn't enough room for a bicycle to go between the black sedan and the car next to it.

I was only a few seconds away from the inevitable collision and was still traveling quite rapidly. My last thought was to slam into a parked car, but it was too late, as my arms tightened on the steering wheel and I froze. My stomach rose up to my throat. I stopped breathing as I braced myself for the moment of impact. I was resigned to the ripping and tearing of metal, and the smashing of glass, but there was no bump, no impact, no collision.

For a split second, the street became dark as night. It was a greenish darkness. I could see the outline of the front hood of my car penetrating the dark, greenish trunk of the vehicle in front of me.

There was no sound of a crash, and the two human figures in front did not appear to move or even flinch. They disappeared from view. I felt like I was floating through this green darkness with my hands still glued tightly to the steering wheel. I had a sensation of passing right through the other car.

The darkness abruptly changed back to bright sunny daylight. As I glanced into my rearview mirror, I was astounded to see the black sedan still waiting in the same spot. But now it was behind me. How could that be?

As soon as traffic cleared, the mysterious black sedan completed its turn and drove on down a side street with both occupants staring straight ahead, completely ignoring me as if I didn't exist. I wanted to swing around and follow that car to find out what was going on, but with no brakes I still had a problem to solve.

The next city block was free of parked cars. While still coasting, I started edging my car as close as possible toward the high curb. Luckily for me, there were several piles of raked leaves along the curb, and I kept plowing into them, which helped me to slow down. Then the high cement curb grabbed my right front tire and brought me to an abrupt stop.

I shut off the engine and rested my head in both hands, breathing heavily as I said out loud, "My God! What happened back there?" I knew I wasn't traveling fast enough to go over the top of the mysterious sedan. I certainly couldn't go under it, and there wasn't enough room to go around it.

Did I really go through it?

Slowly, I got out of the Studebaker. I still looked back down the street, trying to see if I could spot the black sedan again. My legs felt weak and wobbly. I was still shaking from the whole incident.

I was several blocks away from a public telephone, but there were several homes on either side of the street. I started knocking on doors until I found a kindly woman who let me use her telephone to call my boss and advise him of my plight. He told me to stay right there with the car until he could send a tow truck for me.

A short time later the tow truck arrived, and the driver was kind enough to drop me off at the Y.M.C.A. where I was living. On our way downtown, the driver asked me what happened to my car.

I started to say that I drove through another vehicle, but I could tell by his facial expression that he wouldn't believe me, so I just told him that my brakes failed. I also knew I couldn't tell my boss what really happened.

For years I kept silent about the incident, but I could never forget it.

As we approached downtown Cleveland on the expressway, we caught up with the tail end of the usual traffic jam. I hate to think what would have happened to me a half hour earlier if I had come charging down here with a car that had no brakes. That mysterious phantom auto saved me from a disaster.

—*Herb Barlow, FATE contributing writer*

Vortexes, Time slips, and Portals to Other Dimensions

If Einstein were still around today, what would his genius intellect be able to infer about the strange subjects of vortexes, portals, and other dimensions? While the greatest minds in science have attempted to make heads or tails of some the greatest riddles of physics, people have been sending stories to *FATE* magazine for decades, chronicling what may be the answers to those very riddles.

While we enjoy a freedom of mobility on the Earth, there are special sacred places that purportedly have the ability to transport people and objects through time and space with ease. The great curves of infinite space and the unabashed trajectory of time work in collusion to confound people with episodes of missing time and journeys that defy logic. Take, for instance, the incredible story of a husband and wife out collecting flowers one oddly snowy day when suddenly the husband disappears into another dimension as easily as Alice fell down the rabbit hole. Or the chilling experience of one woman whose comatose visions led her to a realm of existence filled with bright flowering lights and objects flying about like UFOs. The following stories represent those rare instances assembled by *FATE* for the scrutinizing eyes of all those searching for the answers to questions of what lies beyond this dimension.

Teleported Pillbox

Some time ago, I was preparing to go to the laundromat in Boerne, Texas, and I put the necessary dimes into a little butterfly-ornamented, gold pillbox. The laundromat was crowded that used the dimes, so I set the pillbox on the table where several women were folding their clean clothes. As I was about to leave, I remembered my pillbox, but I could not find it anywhere. I searched the table, my purse, and the floor and finally decided someone must have inadvertently folded it in her clothes.

Almost in tears, I left. That had been given to me by my son's girl. I was very fond of it, not only of its beauty, but because it was a cherished gift.

When I arrived home I sat for a moment on the edge of my bed and addressed God, telling Him that I was asking for something that was mine, it was a gift of love. I cleared a little place on the table before me and fervently asked that the pillbox be placed there.

I proceeded to fold my clothes and put them away. When I turned around, my lovely pillbox was waiting for me on the table.

—*Molly Anstiss, Boerne, Tex.*

An Unexpected Journey

The early part of April 1966 brought some decent weather to England, but suddenly in the middle of the month, spring did an about-face. I awoke one morning to find a blizzard raging. I knew the snow would concern my wife, for she had agreed to arrange some floral decorations for an important charity event. We live near Poole in Dorset, far south enough that the snow soon melted, but it hadn't done the spring blossoms much good.

About a half-mile away from our house runs a broad avenue, richly lined with trees and rhododendrons. Years ago this was an exclusive residential district where beautiful mansions stood, but now many have been pulled down and apartment buildings have gone up in their stead.

Alongside one large block of flats, three vacant lots of considerable acreage have been left untended and over the years have reverted to natural growth. My wife suggested that we look there for flowering shrubs or some growth she might use for her project.

We were walking down the center of the open space toward the flats and about halfway, my wife spotted a large flowering cherry tree amid the scrub and went over to collect a few branches. I told her to call out if she needed help and I would go on. We both saw clumps of primroses nearby, amazed that these wild flowers had found their way to this forlorn spot.

My wife turned to the left toward the cherry tree. I stood where I was a moment, looking up at the flats and back again to the primroses.

When I raised my eyes again toward the apartment building it was gone! Everything else seemed perfectly normal; I could see my wife in the distant bushes. But the flats simply were not there!

It dawned on me that this was an amazing experience. I have had many vivid experiences of entering another dimension during sleep, and most of us recognize the intangible "frontier" between materiality and fantasy in the dream state. But this was quite different.

Then something else happened. Everything changed; a vast open nothingness surrounded me. But I had not lost my orientation because the sun was shining and gave me my bearings. But had I entered another dimension? And would I get out? The "exit" must be my point of entry, I thought, so I crossed two sticks on the ground to mark my position. Then I walked on to the place where the flats should have been and on and on. No flats, no road, no traffic—just a vast open space and no sign of any kind of life.

I suddenly remembered my wife would be sorely worried about me and retraced my steps, right through where the flats should have been, to my marker of crossed sticks. I saw my wife near me, so I spoke to her. She jumped, saying, "How you startled me! Where have you been? I called you and searched for you and couldn't find you." Then she saw my marker and asked, "What is the witches' cross for? Have you been up to something? You look very guilty."

I calmed her by saying I had indulged in a little experiment.

She wanted one more look around before we left with the branches she had collected and this gave me time to reconnoiter a bit. Everything was back to normal, it seemed. The apartment building stood where it belonged and the scrub bushes and trees and rubbish again were visible. But I found one odd thing. The ground where I had been standing was soft and bare. I could see my footprints going toward the flats but they suddenly ended as if I had stepped off the ground into thin air! And my return path started in the same manner as the outgoing marks suddenly had vanished!

Oddly enough, this experience seemed to me a sequel to dreams I have had of a devastated world and deserted cities. But the question remains: had I stepped into the past, the future or another space dimension?

—J. P. J. Chapman, Poole, Dorset, England

Highway in the Sky

My baby girl Lorelei was born by caesarean section on September 27, 1957, in Fayette Memorial Hospital, Connersville, Indiana. My doctor, W. A. Kemp, was pleased with my progress and when Lorelei was eight days old, he removed the stitches in my incision and arranged to release me from the hospital.

All my life I have had the habit of keeping my hands scrupulously clean and this may have saved my life. In preparing to go home, I scrubbed them thoroughly and while standing before the lavatory, I felt a tearing sensation in the lower part of my abdomen. I walked slowly to a rocking chair beside my hospital bed and sat down clasping my hands over my incision. A warm wetness on my hands made me look down—to my horror I saw that my shortie hospital gown and robe were bright with blood. Pulling aside the robe and gown, I literally caught my spilling guts in my hands.

Fortunately a nurse walked into my room just then and I called to her, "Come and see what has happened!"

The second surgery required four and a half hours. Dr. Kemp had to replace and reroute all my insides, it seemed. He told my husband Franklin that I had a 50 percent chance to survive; there was great danger of infection and my intestines were hopelessly mixed up.

My body lay unconscious for three days—October 5, 6, and 7—but my spirit was elsewhere. It was traveling a great highway in the sky. Sometimes I sat beside the highway and watched other persons coming and going. Some had an angelic appearance and floated among the people as if on wings.

Somehow I knew that those who were walking back and forth were waiting for something, as I was, so I sat quietly and watched them. I believed we were all just outside Heaven, for nearby I could see a high, glittering wall with a massive closed gate. I looked upward and saw many strange objects flying over us. I thought of the many different ways UFOs have been described. These were in different shapes and one particularly interested me. It was oblong and very large. In big letters on its side were printed the words: "Mother Ship."

In the incredibly beautiful scenery of many colors—especially white, blue, and silver—I felt comfortable as I sat watching. I was sad only when my children came to mind. I was most concerned about the youngest ones and particularly the beautiful little baby lying in the hospital nursery. How I longed to hold her again! But I felt I never would see any of them again. Then suddenly the big "Mother Ship" came near and a voice from inside called, "Come along! You are going home."

I awoke in the hospital, severely chilled. My teeth were chattering and I was shaking so much that I could hardly ring for the nurse. I told her I was freezing to death. She gave me some kind of injection and then wrapped me in warm blankets. I immediately dropped off into a natural refreshing sleep.

When I awakened the next time I was starving but otherwise I felt fine. My doctor came to my bedside smiling. He said, "Well, Cleo, I guess you're going to live!"

—*Cleo Mills, Connersville, Ind.*

Mind Over Space:
The Mystery of Teleportation

We have reached a point at which the problem of human transportation no longer is a matter of calm contemplation of legend and folklore, but a violent assault against logical and scientific thinking. The claims to these mysterious happenings do not die as we reach the experimental age, but rather multiply and unfold more fully attested. Moreover, for the source of the power that accomplishes transportation, we have seen the spirits of the dead brought in by spiritualists.

Whether one approves of Spiritualism as a religion, psychic science, or psychotherapy, the new approach has had the tremendous advantage of making transportation a near-laboratory phenomenon. We find it recurring under generally the same conditions with the same *dramatis personae* in the presence of increasingly more numerous witnesses.

But we also find, perhaps as a psychological check to a state of affairs gravely disturbing orthodox thinking, the theory that the actors in the transportation drama disappear via the fourth dimension in much the same way that a hypothetical two-dimensional object (possessing length and breadth only) would transcend the boundaries of a circle by being lifted up into the third dimension (of height) and deposited again on the two-dimensional plane outside the circle. On the two-dimensional level of existence, the object would vanish and reappear mysteriously at another point in space.

This hyperspace theory does not bar an extraneous agency, to which the fourth dimension might be a sporting ground or native habitat, but it eliminates thinking of divine intervention, of a magical act, or of the agency of the Devil or Poltergeist. On the basis of this theory, transportation might be due to a knack of fourth-dimensional functioning, haphazard, unconscious or willed, or it might be accidental due to a warp or fault in space (an idea which we meet frequently in science-fiction). If persons do fall through a hole in space, we would have the advantage of being able to explain what happens to those who do not return. They may fail to find the entrance point, like a man who falls into a frozen river through a hole and is carried away by his own momentum or by the current underneath the sheet of ice.

—*Nandor Fodor, FATE contributing writer*

How Lost Was My Father

In the afternoon of September 23, 1880, David Lang, a farmer living near Gallatin, Tennessee, spoke to his wife on the porch of their home and then walked away across a 40-acre field. He was fully visible to his wife and to his two young children, who were playing near the porch.

Meanwhile, August Peck, a Gallatin lawyer, and his brother-in-law were driving up in a horse-drawn buggy along the road in front of the house. Peck, who had come to see Lang on business, noticed him crossing the field while still a quarter of a mile away and drew air into his lungs to call out.

Lang was in the in middle of the field, the grass of which had been cropped short by horses.

There were no obstructing stones or trees. He was in full view of three pairs of adult eyes. At that precise moment, he disappeared with an abruptness that made Peck think the ground had caved in under him.

The surface of the field, however, was unbroken. Peck, his brother-in-law, and Lang's hysterical wife searched every inch of it. They found nothing to show where or how Lang had disappeared. Later that day, neighbors also searched without result. For weeks afterward the field was crowded with the well-meaning and the curious, but no trace of Lang was found. A county surveyor said there was no possibility of a cave-in as limestone bedrock lay a few feet under the soil of the field.

A strange feature of the case is that, although Lang had vanished utterly from the familiar world, he evidently was not quite out of touch with it. The following spring his two children, George, 8, and Emma, 11, noticed that in the middle of the field where their father had disappeared was an irregular circle of rank grass some 15 feet in diameter. Horses avoided the grass within the circle, as did grasshoppers, ants, and other insects.

On a sudden impulse as she stood at the edge of the circle, Emma called out to her father. George joined her. They called repeatedly and were about to leave when the incredible happened. Faint and far-off, they heard the voice of a man calling for help—a voice that Emma was certain was her father's. She told the experience to her mother, who said she also had heard the voice. However, the fact that it had grown farther and fainter each day had led her to abandon any hope it might have held out.

If Lang indeed had fallen into a hole in space, and if time in his new habitat paralleled that here, he evidently managed to survive for several months. During this period, he must have searched constantly for the point at which he had entered—and failed to find it.

The idea that there may be a knack of fourth-dimensional functioning was first put forward in psychical research by F. W. H. Myers in his great book, *Human Personality and its Survival of Bodily Death*. He coined a rather formidable term for it: "psychorrhagic diathesis." By it he meant a breaking loose of elements of the human psyche that have the ability of affecting space. (I have discussed the significance of I this as a comprehensive alternate theory for the understanding of psychic phenomena in "Inversion of Time and Space," Light, Dec. 25, 1934.) The idea was not appreciated at the time when it was broached. Yet it contains the germ of a momentous theory. It well may be that the phenomenon of human transportation may force upon us the hypothesis that at times, in states of trance and ecstasy, an energy is released from the unconscious which enables us to transcend the limitations of three-dimensional space.

Sir Ernest Wallis Budge, the great authority on ancient Egypt and Chaldea, formerly keeper of the mummies in the British Museum, declared in an interview given to the Daily Express on January 17, 1934:

> I knew an African and an Indian who could vanish into air as you spoke to them, touched them. Like the Cheshire cat in Alice in Wonderland, first they were there, then there was only the grin, then that, too, disappeared. It was no question of hypnotism, for I walked through the spot where they had been standing. In the same way they would reappear, and, as they solidified, push me away.

There was a hue and cry because of this interview, and Budge was forced to declare it as unauthorized. The wording that as they solidified they pushed him away suggests that these persons knew how to find the same hole in space through which they disappeared.

In the now-defunct Ghost Club of London, I heard the story of a personal experience of the same nature by Captain Pierce, a man of wide interests and travels. It happened in the Canadian backwoods, but how it occurred was never quite clear to him. Something came over him just as he looked at his wristwatch. A moment later he was in new and strange surroundings, 100 miles from the spot where he looked at his watch. The travel of which he had no conscious knowledge was absolutely instantaneous, and he felt none the worse for the experience.

Jean Durant, a 24-year-old French Canadian whose story is dated 1898, claimed control over the phenomenon, until one day he lost it and was never seen again. I take the story from an article by Ray Preedy in *Guide and Ideas*, London, November 14, 1936.

According to this article, three doctors tested Durant's claim that he could disappear from a locked room and appear in the next one. A man named Williams gave a signed and sworn testimony that he actually had seen Durant fade away into nothingness, his dressing gown collapsing and falling down on the floor. But Durant became ill after his experience and put it down to being watched. (It means that being rendered self-conscious inhibits that which is purely unconscious.)

Hence, in subsequent tests by medical men and the police, Durant demanded that only the door of the cell in which he was locked should be kept under observation. In these tests, Preedy says, Durant sometimes was secured with handcuffs and fastened to the cell wall with a heavy length of chain, the door being sealed at a half-dozen points with wax. Yet he appeared suddenly among the watchers. The handcuffs were on the floor, the lock on them intact, and the seals on the door unbroken.

Finally, Durant was invited to a demonstration in Chicago. His arms and legs were pinioned and the cell door closed and sealed. This time he failed to appear. After an hour's waiting the cell was opened. The rope and handcuffs were on the floor, but Durant was gone and nobody ever saw or heard of him again.

How did Durant do it? We have a hint in the statement of a doctor who, before Durant appeared at his side, heard sounds of, heavy breathing from the far side of the door. It sounded like a man in deep sleep. From this we may assume that Durant, like so many others, went into a state of trance, and what happened after that was beyond his control. As he had no misadventure before, he did not expect any, but apparently he trusted his luck too far.

That the need of self-preservation may be a motive behind transportation, appears from an interview with Mrs. Kathleen Barkel, published in Light, January 19, 1934, in which she speaks of a weird adventure in a crowded shopping district of West Croydon:

> *While walking with a friend, I was apparently*
> *hit by a motorcar. I felt a concussion. The next*

moment I found myself in the doorway of a shop some distance away. On recovering my senses, I turned back and saw that a crowd had collected around the motorcar. They were looking for a body, which had mysteriously disappeared. My friend was in an agony. When I walked up to her, she just gaped at me. Apparently, at the moment that I was hit by the car I bounced off, unseen by anyone, like a rubber ball and experienced instantaneous transportation.

D. D. Home, the famous medium, narrates a similar incident in a letter to the editor of the *Spiritual Magazine* (1861, p. 61). He was staying at the Chateau de Cercay, half an hour from Paris, and went hunting in the park. The game used to go for shelter to an immense poplar tree. Toward this he advanced cautiously.

When close up to it, I was raising my head to look for in my game when on my right I heard someone call out, "Here, here!" My only feeling was surprise at being thus suddenly addressed in English. Desire to have a good look out for my game overruled my curiosity as to whom the exclamation had come from; I was continuing to raise my head to the level of the hedge, when suddenly I was seized by the collar of my coat and vest and lifted off the ground; at the same instant I heard a crashing sound, and then all was quiet.

I felt neither fear nor wonder. My first thought was that by some accident my gun had exploded, and that I was in the spirit land; but, looking about, I saw that I was still in the material world—there was the gun still in my hand.

My attention was then drawn to what appeared to be a tree immediately before me, where no tree had been. On examination this proved to be the fallen limb of the high tree under which I was standing. I then saw that I had been drawn aside from this fallen limb a distance of six or seven feet. I ran, in my excitement, as fast as I could to the chateau ....

The limb which had thus fallen measured sixteen yards and a half in length, and where it had broken from the trunk, it was one yard in circumference. The part of the limb which struck the very spot where I had been standing, measured 24 inches in circumference, and penetrated the earth at least a foot.

The incident, at best, is a case of levitation, a very frequent occurrence with D. D. Home, but it is worth including here as, together with Mrs. Barkel's story, it may establish self-preservation as a trigger that releases the energy with which transportation is accomplished. The same unconscious need was operative in the case of Apollonius of Tyana when he is said to have saved himself from the wrath of Emperor Domitian by disappearing.

When the question of the fourth-dimension was brought up by Professor Zollner of Leipzig, Lazar von Hellenbach asked his medium whether a human being could disappear by way of that dimension. The answer was "a human being could, under certain conditions. There is too much respect for it to do it often, but there are cases when human beings disappeared and became invisible to the persecutors, as did Christ in the Temple." (Willie Reichel: *Occult Experiences*, p. 28)

Hints at the dynamics of the transition into another dimension might be found in some transportation instances quoted by Charles Fort in his book, *Lo* (Victor Gollanez edition, London, 1931): "According to the Courrier de l'Isere, two little girls, last of December 1842, were picking leaves from the ground, near Clavaux (Livet), France, when they saw stones falling around them. The stones fell with uncanny slowness. The children ran to their homes, and told of the phenomenon, and returned with their parents. Again stones fell, and with the same uncanny 'slowness.' It is said that relatively to these falls the children were attractive agents. There was another phenomenon, an upward current into which the children were dragged, as if into a vortex. We might have had data of mysterious disappearances of children, but the parents, who were unaffected by the current, pulled them back." (p. 27)

Instead of a vortex, we find the victims dragged downward into a hole in the following instance:

"Early in the morning of December 9th, 1873, Thomas B. Cumpston and his wife 'who occupied good positions in Leeds' were arrested in a railroad station, in Bristol, England, charged with disorderly conduct, both of them in their nightclothes, Cumpston having fired a pistol. See the London Times, Dec. 11, 1873. Cumpston excitedly told that he and his wife had arrived the day before, from Leeds, and had taken a room in a Bristol hotel, and that, early in the morning, the floor had 'opened,' and that, as he was about to be dragged into the 'opening,' his wife had saved him, both of them becoming so terrified that they had jumped out of the window, running to the railroad station, looking for a policeman. In the Bristol Daily Post, Dec. 10, is an account of proceedings in the police court. Cumpston's excitement was still so intense that he could not clearly express himself. Mrs. Cumpston testified that, early in the evening, both of them had been alarmed by loud sounds, but that they had been reassured by the landlady. At three or four in the morning the sounds were heard again. They jumped out on the floor, which was felt giving way under them. Voices repeating their exclamations were heard, or their own voices echoed strangely. Then, according to what she saw, or thought she saw, the floor opened wide. Her husband was falling into this 'opening,' when she dragged him back." (p. 188)

"In the Sunday Express, London, Dec. 5, 1926, Lieut. Col. Foley tells of an occurrence that resembles the Cumpstons' experience. A room in Corpus Christi College (Cambridge University) was, in Oct. 1904, said to be haunted. Four students, of whom Shane Leslie, the writer, was one, investigated. Largely the story is of an invisible, but tangible, thing, or being, which sometimes became dimly visible, inhabiting, or visiting, this room. The four students went into the room, and one of them was dragged away from the others. His companions grabbed him. 'Like some powerful magnet' something was drawing him out of their grasp. They pulled against it, and fought in frenzy, and they won the tug. Other students, outside the room, were shouting. Undergraduates came running down the stairs, and crowding into the room, wrecked it, even tearing out the oak paneling. Appended to the story, in the Sunday Express, is a statement by Mr. Leslie —'Col. Foley has given an accurate account of the occurrence.'" (p. 189)

Fort uses the word teleportation instead of transportation. He is anxious to dissociate himself from spiritualistic or ghostly agencies. He quotes a report from the New York World, March 25, 1883, according to which the daughter of Jesse Miller, of Greenville Township, Somerset Co., Pa., was "transported several times out of the house into the front yard," and adds: "But it was her belief that apparitions were around and most of our data are not concerned with ghostly appearances." (p. 182) Similarly, as told in the Cambrian Daily Leader (Swansea, Wales), July 7, 1887, "poltergeist phenomena were occurring in the home of the Rev. David Phillips, of Swansea ... A woman of Mr. Phillips' household had been transported over a wall, and back toward a brook, where she arrived in a 'semi-conscious condition.' I note, that not in agreement with our notions on teleportation, it was this woman's belief that an apparition had carried her." (p. 183)

Franz Hartmann, as an occultist, did not believe in transportation by spirits because such power of spirits did not fit into his philosophy. Fort, too, has his own system in which teleportation is a basic fact by which many otherwise unexplainable happenings can be explained. He says of stone throwing in poltergeist cases: "It may be that somebody, gifted with what we think we mean by 'agency,' fiercely hates somebody else, he can, out of intense visualization, direct, by teleportation, bombardment of stones upon his enemy." (p. 41)

Nakedness dreams, according to Fort, may be due to the fact that "occult transportations of human beings do occur, and that, because of their selectiveness, clothes are sometimes not included." This thought is based on newspaper reports of strange naked men appearing at some places, bewildered and lost. He assumes that in such cases the dreamer woke up before he was teleported back.

The feeling of déjà vu (strange familiarity with a place as if we had seen it before), Fort places under this theory also: "It may be that many persons have been teleported back and forth, without knowing it, or without having more than the dimmest impression of the experience."

When people claim to have seen a ghost that had vanished, he thinks the observers have seen a real man in the first phase of teleportation. "So many ghosts in white garments have been reported because persons, while asleep, have been teleported in their nightclothes." (p. 186)

Apparitions of the living are to be understood in the same vein. When persons have been seen "far from where, as far as those persons themselves knew, they were at the time … human beings have been switched away somewhere, and soon switched back." (p. 187)

To explain teleportation as a basic fact, Fort advances this speculation: "It looks to me that, throughout what is loosely called Nature, teleportation exists, as a means of distribution of things and materials, and that sometimes human beings have command, mostly unconsciously, though sometimes as a development from research and experiment, of this force. It is said that in savage tribes there are 'rain makers,' and it may be that among savages there are teleportationists." (p. 41)

This is a fascinating notion and a few things could be said in its favor. For untold ages, before we invented radio, insects had antennae and communicated by wireless waves. Teleportation of objects may be essentially an electronic problem. If it exists solved in nature, the technical solution may not be an unattainable dream. But Fort claims more than that. He endows Nature with a form of psychic life that reminds one of ancient notions of the existence of a planetary spirit. At that point his philosophy tails into sheer mysticism.

—*Stuart Palmer, FATE contributing writer*

A Night in Another Dimension

In October 1979 when Len and Cynthia Gisby and their friends Geoff and Pauline Simpson, all of Dover, England, decided to take a trip they certainly had no way of knowing precisely how far away they would be going. In fact, they were heading straight for one of the most baffling holidays of modern times.

Geoff Simpson, a railway worker, then 44, and his wife, then 45, and a cleaner at a social club, were quite excited when Len and Cynthia Gisby invited them to go along on their holiday trip. The plan was to take the ferry across the English Channel and drive through France to northern Spain for two weeks of late-summer sunshine. Indeed, it all worked out perfectly. The weather was fine and the ride through the strange countryside was packed with interest.

On October 3, around 9:30 p.m., they were on the autoroute (freeway) north of Montelimar, France, far to the south. It had been a pleasant day, but they were tired and the encroaching darkness led them to look for a place to stay. Ahead loomed a plush motel, and after a short discussion they decided to stop there for the night.

When Len went inside, he was confronted in the lobby by a man dressed in a rather strange plum-colored uniform. But he presumed this to be part of the local custom. The man informed Len that unfortunately there was no room at the motel. "However, " Len was told, "if you take the road off the autoroute there"—and he pointed south—"then you will find a small hotel. They will have rooms."

Len thanked the man and his party drove away. The last faint traces of daylight still painted the sky when they found the road indicated. As they drove on Cynthia and Pauline commented on the old buildings lining the roadside. The posters plastered on them were promoting a circus. "It was a very old-fashioned circus," Pauline remarked. "That's why we took so much interest."

The men were more interested in the road itself, cobbled and very narrow. When no other traffic passed by, they began to doubt the wisdom of this plan. But suddenly Cynthia spotted some lights and they pulled to a halt in front of a building by the roadside. It was long and low, with a row of brightly lit windows. There were some men standing in front of it. Cynthia got out but came back to the car saying, "It's not a hotel. It's an inn." So they drove on, past a long border of trees, which now lined the road.

Presently, they reached two other buildings. One appeared to be a police station. The other had a sign saying "Hotel." Thankful that their journey was over, Len got out and went to ask for accommodations. He came back sighing with relief, "They have rooms. " And so the tired travelers unloaded their bags. It was about 10:00 p.m.; they estimated it had taken them about 10 minutes to reach the hotel from the autoroute motel. The hotel itself was a curious ranch-style building. It had just two stories and looked quaint and old-fashioned. As they entered two boys were just leaving.

Because none of the four spoke French and the hotel manager apparently spoke no English, they made themselves known as best they could and were shown to their rooms. On the way they noticed that the building's interior was as strange as its exterior.

Everything was old and made of heavy wood. There were no tablecloths on the tables in the dining room and some men in rough clothes sat drinking around one table near the bar. There seemed to be no telephones, elevators, or other modern equipment anywhere.

Upstairs in their rooms even odder delights awaited them. The beds were large but had no pillows, only bolsters. The sheets were heavy. The mattresses seemed to sag in the middle but felt comfortable enough to lie on. Besides, it was too late to go anywhere else. The doors had no locks, just wooden catches. And the two couples had to share a bathroom with old-fashioned plumbing and soap attached to a metal bar stuck in the wall.

"Look at this funny soap," Geoff kept chuckling.

After unpacking they went down to the dining room for a meal. Although unable to understand the menu, they did recognize the word *oeuf* (egg) and ordered four of that dish. After they had drunk lager from tankards supplied to them, their dinners arrived on huge heavy plates. Included with the eggs were steak and french-fried potatoes. Their meal finished, they drank more lager. The girl who served them could not understand English either, so they did not speak.

Satisfied with their meal and facing another long journey the next day, they went straight to bed. It took no time at all for them to fall asleep.

Morning woke them early; sunlight filtered in through the windows, which had no glass in them, just wooden shutters. Pauline removed the chair she had wedged against the door because she was afraid to sleep without some way of holding the door shut. They dressed and went back down to the dining room for breakfast. This simple meal consisted of bread, jam, and coffee. "The coffee tasted black and horrible," Geoff recalls with disgust. While they were eating, a woman came into the room and sat down opposite them. She wore a silk evening gown and carried a dog under her arm. "It was strange," Pauline says. "It looked like she had just come in from a ball, but it was seven in the morning! I couldn't take my eyes off her."

Then two *gendarmes* (police officers) arrived, wearing deep blue uniforms and capes and large peaked hats. "They were nothing like the gendarmes we saw anywhere else in France," Geoff says. "Their uniforms seemed to be very old."

As they finished breakfast, they all decided they wanted some souvenir of this unusual hotel. They did not think of it as anything other than a charming rural place that would be a delight to talk about when they got home. So Geoff took his camera into the room and photographed Pauline standing by the shuttered windows. Len, while out packing his car, took a photograph of Cynthia inside the hotel silhouetted against the window.

Then, to be certain of at least one good shot, he took another one. His camera was sophisticated and had an automatic winder.

Len and Geoff decided to ask the gendarmes, who were still there talking to the manager, the best way to take the autoroute to Avignon and the Spanish border, but the policemen shrugged at the word "autoroute" and plainly did not know the term. Geoff presumed that Len's attempts at French dialect were just not successful.

Eventually the gendarmes understood that the travelers wished to go to Spain and directed them to the old Avignon road. From what little knowledge of the local geography they had, this seemed a long way round to the two Englishmen and they resolved to go back to the Montelimar autoroute by the way they had come.

With the car packed and three companions ready to leave, Len went across to the manager and asked for the bill. The man scribbled a sum on a piece of paper and showed it to the rather astonished tourist. It read 19 francs (about $3.00).

"No, no," Len motioned. "For all four of us."

The manager simply nodded. When Len indicated that they had eaten a meal, the manager continued to nod. Len showed the piece of paper to the gendarmes who smiled and indicated that it was quite correct. Without further ado, Len paid up in cash and they left.

"Come on," Geoff remembers whispering. "Let's get out of here before he changes his mind."

The day was hot and sunny and they traveled the tree-lined road back to the autoroute quite easily. Again it was deserted of traffic until they joined the road toward Spain. Then, forgetting all about the hotel, they went on to pass a very happy two weeks in Spain.

On the drive back, naturally, the four decided to stop at the same hotel. Not many places offered such unique service at such phenomenal prices. The weather was miserable, with rain bucketing down, but they found the turnoff easily and drove down it.

"There are the circus signs," Pauline called out. "This is definitely the right road. "

But there was no hotel. They were concerned enough to return to the motel on the autoroute and ask directions. Not only did the man there know of no such hotel but he denied any knowledge of the man in the plum-colored uniform who had directed them to it previously.

Three times they drove up and down the road. But there was no hotel! It had vanished into thin air.

By this time Cynthia was upset and crying. "It has to be here! It can't just disappear like that," she said.

Somebody else suggested it had been knocked down. "At those prices they probably went broke," one person speculated.

"They couldn't do that in two weeks. Not without a trace," Geoff concluded.

They finally gave up the hunt. Shaking their heads, they drove on north to Lyon and a hotel there. Bed, breakfast, and evening meal for four, with admittedly rather more modern facilities, cost them 247 francs (about $40).

The Gisbys and the Simpsons were mildly intrigued by their adventure, but it never crossed their minds to invest the story with a paranormal explanation until their holiday snapshots arrived back. Geoff had a 20-exposure Kodak film and had taken it to a local chain store. Len had a 36-exposure film, which had been processed by the manufacturer.

The three photographs of the hotel (one by Geoff, two by Len) had all been taken in the middle of the respective films. But none of the hotel shots were returned. What's more, there were no spoiled negatives. Each film had its full quota of photographs. It was as if the pictures that they all clearly remember taking did not exist; they had disappeared into limbo just like the hotel!

Utterly baffled and confused, the four resolved to tell only their families and friends. Geoff, raised in Rochdale, Lancashire, visited his home in January 1980 and told his family. When I talked with them in 1985, they smiled but said, "If anyone else had told us we would have laughed. We still chuckled but we knew it had to be true."

A fashion-conscious friend discussed the uniforms with Len and pointed out from a book that gendarmes did wear the kind he was describing—prior to 1905! One or two persons suggested that they had experienced a "time slip" and stayed at a hotel that existed around the turn of the century. Len and Cynthia thought this idea made sense. Geoff and Pauline preferred to forget the whole thing.

But unbeknown to them, one person they talked to actually worked for the local newspaper in Dover. Three years after the events, she published their tale and the cat was finally out of the bag. From then on the publicity bandwagon began to roll.

Looking back, in July 1985, Geoff was philosophical. "We never wanted the publicity," he said. "We just wanted to forget it. But once it happened, then we all wanted to go back and try again to find that hotel.

"This trip is the only thing we ever got out of it. A local TV station made a drama about it, but we never got paid. They jazzed it up, using actors like Gordon Jackson from *Upstairs Downstairs*. For instance, when it came to the photographs, they had us taking one picture of the group of us standing in front of the hotel. That never happened. Then, in the film, when the picture came back, we were in it but the hotel wasn't. That's just eye-wash. Why do they do things like that?"

In 1984 Yorkshire Television, filming the series Arthur C. Clarke's *World of Strange Powers*, flew the four of them to Lyon and then filmed reconstructed attempts to find the hotel. "They set it all up by getting the police to pretend to call the tourist board. But we did go to the area and look. We even thought we had found the place. But it was not our hotel—just an old house, nothing like the hotel. At the place where we were all sure the hotel had been there was nothing at all."

The French tourist board in Lyon says there is no hotel like the one the Gisbys and Simpsons describe.

Geoff and Pauline were adamant that, apart from this trip, they had never made any money out of their story. "We don't want to," they say. "We just know it happened."

Yorkshire TV personnel say they examined Len Gisby's camera and film negatives.

"There was evidence that the camera had tried to wind on in the middle of the film. Sprocket holes on the negatives showed damage." But of the mysterious photographs there was no trace.

In July 1985, I spent an evening with the Simpsons, in the company of fellow researchers Linda Taylor and Harry Harris. Harris had arranged for the couple to be interviewed and hypnotically regressed by psychiatrist Dr. Albert Keller at his Manchester surgery. Pauline could not be hypnotized, but Geoff Simpson proved an excellent subject, reliving the events with emotion and awe. A detailed description of the adventure was offered, but no new elements were uncovered (or fantasized).

What really happened to the four travelers in rural France? Was this a time slip? If so, one wonders why the hotel manager was apparently not surprised by their futuristic vehicle and clothing and why he accepted their 1979 currency (which certainly would have appeared odd to anybody living that far back in the past). The Simpsons consider these points and have no explanations.

"You tell us what the answer is. We only know what happened," Geoff concludes.

—*Jenny Randles*

Spirit Guides and Angels

Nearly every culture and era throughout the world has told and retold stories of intervention by deities and beings that arrive in times of need. Those are the creatures that seem to hold a stake in the tragedy and triumphs of the lives of man. Whether for good of evil, they still find a way to give warnings and premonitions in order to direct the lives of human beings. One imagines that there must be greater cosmic significance in human life when so many acts of intervention have influenced the lives of man.

We all have a story to share of something terrible happening when we least expect and the miraculous reversal of fortunes that seem to have no rational or logical explanation other than that the watchfulness of some sympathetic intelligence changed the course of our lives. Some people have regarded these encounters as the traditional angel's delivery of the words and warnings of God. Some have reported that loved ones lost to death have appeared to save the lives of those on Earth.

My Blue Angel

During World War II in London, England, I met many people who told strange tales of premonitions that compelled them to leave areas just before death fell from the heavens in the form of bombs. What caused these people to know that danger was imminent?

Because of my own experiences at that time, I am convinced that guardian angels are with us, endeavoring to guide, protect, and impinge their thoughts upon our minds, especially in times of stress and danger.

In 1940 I was living with my mother right in the heart of London, on the top floor of a four-story building. We had an Anderson shelter in the small backyard, but it was much too small for the four families who occupied the building. During the frequent bombing raids, some of them trudged to the crowded Underground Stations at night where they packed in like proverbial sardines. Mother would squeeze into the yard shelter but, after sitting up one night with her in that dark, damp, earthy-smelling "hole of Calcutta," I decided that I would rather take my chances upstairs in my own comfortable bed.

Strict blackout rules were in effect and rigidly enforced. Heavy draperies and tape sealed the windows at night so that when the dimmed lights were extinguished the room was so dark that I could not see my hand even if I held it only one inch in front of my face.

Starting with the very first night that I decided to stay alone in the house, I felt a wonderful peace and protection surrounding me. Even in the utter blackness, I noticed a blue light, which shifted from place to place in the room, but located itself right by the bed when bombs were falling in the vicinity. This blue light remained with me for weeks, all during the "blitz," and I slept, unafraid, through many heavy raids. The house lost its windows innumerable times and the outside walls bore pockmarks left by exploding shrapnel. Yet I knew that I was perfectly safe in my room, the blue light radiated such a strong aura of love and protection.

Finally, one night after saying my prayers and hopping into bed, I felt I must know more about the source of "my" blue light. There was a lull in the almost incessant noise of exploding bombs and I sat up in bed and said, rather hesitantly, "If someone is here, please give me a sign." Immediately I heard three distinct raps on my bedside table and, simultaneously with them, the words "Sister Theresa" were whispered to me.

I am ashamed to disclose that this response to my request alarmed me more than the bombs ever did! I waited a few minutes, but nothing more occurred except that the blue light remained near the bed until I went to sleep.

At this time I had read nothing about mysticism, although other unexplainable things had happened to me from earliest childhood and I often had predicted things that came true. From this time on, I haunted the libraries and read everything I could find on the occult and the psychic. Then one day, noticing a piece in the newspaper about a forthcoming lecture on the occult to be held at the Albert Hall, I made plans to go. I found the lecture most interesting and it whetted my appetite for more knowledge. Something even more wonderfully interesting to me happened at that lecture, something that validated my blue light experience.

At the close of the lecture, an attractive woman approached me, introduced herself and said that she hoped that I had enjoyed the evening. I assured her I had. She hesitated a moment and then continued, "You may not have known it, but you are very psychic. You have had a lovely Nun with you all this evening and her name is Theresa."

Soon after this in June 1941, I was transferred to Hampshire with other personnel of the Bank of England. I led a far more active social life there and eventually met and married my American husband, who has had many remarkable experiences of his own.

From the time that I came to the United States, I never saw my blue light again. I have often joked to friends that my guardian angel missed the plane. But in my heart I feel that she still watches over me and mine and that if I ever need her again she will make herself known—in her very own special way.

—Joan E. Russell, St. Thomas, Virgin Islands

God's Warning Angel

In March 1961, four friends of mine, Patty Miller, Kenneth George, Carroll Larson, and Mary Lou Madsen, were killed in an auto accident two miles east of Maxwell, Iowa; two others with them, Darrell Rench and Dianne Massey, were saved.

The following story was told to me by Charles George who lives in Cambridge, Iowa, eight miles east of Maxwell. Charles George is the father of Kenneth George, who was killed in the wreck.

"On the evening before the accident, my wife and I were getting ready for bed when I heard our dogs barking outside the house. Not wanting them to disturb the neighbors, I went outside to quiet the dogs.

"I could see nothing to cause the dogs to bark, so I headed back to the house. For some reason or other, I happened to glance toward the cemetery (we live four blocks up hill from the cemetery, so I had a good view) and at first I couldn't believe my eyes!

"Directly above the cemetery I saw an angel! It was the most beautiful thing I have ever seen, although I cannot describe it. All around it were multicolored lights.

"I went back in the house and told my wife but she thought I was seeing things.

"Our boy died in the crash the next day.

"All I can think is that this was a warning from God, telling us that we were going to lose someone close to us. Although I never did ask, I have wondered if the parents of the other children in the crash saw anything like I did."

—*Chris Aldrich, Cambridge, Iowa*

Jaws of Death

The narrow, hilly, and crooked roads that I had been following most of the forenoon in September 1955 were becoming a matter of anxiety, especially in the muddy areas. Searching for an unknown individual in that rugged, barren wilderness of Nebraska was indeed a problem.

I finally reached the yard of a considerably neglected ranch. There was no sign of life; however, the double doors of a long, rambling, unpainted machine shed were open. After driving past the old, two-story, apparently deserted house, to within a short distance of the shed, I stopped the car. Approaching the entrance, I called "Hello," thinking someone might be inside.

Instantly, from the darkness within, came a violent, growling scream from a dog. Like a streak straight toward me came the biggest, most vicious, meanest looking German shepherd I ever had ever seen. My first impression was that of a satanic entity tearing out from the depths of Hades.

Black hair bristling the full length of his back, eyes glaring like those of an enraged wolf, saliva drooling from his wide open mouth, lips savagely drawn back showing long glistening white fangs, he came straight toward me.

Men's voices yelled in frantic desperation, "Look out! The dog will kill you!"

I never will forget the terrifying scream of that animal as he lunged.

But suddenly I felt enfolded in a warm, wonderful, courageous peace. Although fully aware that I was about to be attacked and killed by this huge dog, I somehow was unafraid.

In midair, as he leaped toward me, the dogs jaw suddenly snapped shut. His body struck my shoulder, sending me reeling backward, but otherwise I was unharmed. The dog then turned and, with muffled, whimpering sounds, came slowly back to me. He licked my hands. Finally he stretched out on the ground, as if completely exhausted.

The two men who had come running were terribly shaken. After gaining composure, one asked, "What did you do to that dog?"

I said, "I did nothing to him."

Looking at the penitent dog on the ground, he said, "We expected to see you torn to pieces."

The second man, not disguising his bewilderment, said, "I never have seen anything like it. You must have done something."

Did that enraged dog encounter a protecting spirit?
Did he see my guardian angel?

—Henry Burdick, Des Moines, Iowa.

Angel of the Abyss

My mother, Ethel Puckett Damerell, was born in Torquay, England. She grew up there in a fine old house overlooking the English Channel. Atop the cliffs they could feel the salt spray that drifted up whenever there was a storm. The pounding waves broke on the rocks far below and, farther out, the channel would be gray and white with churning water and spume. More frequent however, were the periods of calm beauty when the water was dimpled green and yellow in endless swells, when sea birds rode down the curves.

Torquay was a very quiet town, but it had a number of ghosts, which appears to be usual for England. Mother often told me about family Angels as she called them, and she told me this story concerning her own personal Angel.

In the warm summer months, afternoon tea was taken on a balcony and Mother and Nanny Jones ate their little cakes and sipped their tea and, watched the moods of the channel. There was only the lowest of iron railings about the edge of the balcony but no accident ever had occurred.

Then one night when Mother was eight or nine years old, she walked in her sleep. After this Nanny Jones was terrified lest she repeat her performance and plunge off the cliff. A heavy lock was put on the French doors and every night at bedtime they were locked up and the key was placed in a pocket of Nanny's white apron.

The next summer, Nanny's vacation time came and a substitute came in for the month she was to be gone. She was lectured repeatedly about the doors but, being young and unafraid, she forgot the rule one night, a week after Nanny left. Of course, that was the time Mother walked in her sleep again—for the first time in almost a year.

Her bare foot must have given the iron grill a whack because she instantly woke from the pain. But having tripped against the low railing she found herself falling forward toward the rocks and the sea. Suddenly she was pulled back by strong hands. She peered down at her foot and in the dark barely made out that it was bleeding. Then she looked up into Nanny Jones' face.

Frightened and confused, believing the old nurse had returned unexpectedly, she allowed herself to be led, limping, back to bed. Her foot was examined and made to stop bleeding. She was tucked into bed and fondly chucked under the chin.

"You will never fall while I watch," said Nanny. Then she disappeared in a mist, which Mother said she took for fog creeping up from the channel. The gas lamp, turned very low as a night light, showed the alternate girl nanny sleeping soundly in the other bed, but Mother said, although she felt confused, she soon went to sleep.

The next morning, on the strength of Mother's story and the bruised and swollen foot, the girl was discharged. The entire family now waited for Nanny Jones' return, or at least for a postal card from her. Instead a black-bordered letter arrived. Mother's beloved nurse had died suddenly on the same night she had appeared on the rose balcony.

Then one night about six years later, when Mother was 15 years old and the edge of the family's grief at the loss of Nanny had worn off, a tremendous storm roared in the channel. The high barricade, which had been erected after Mother had been saved from falling by Nanny Jones, was smashed to pieces. As it came crashing down, Mother leaped from her bed and stared through the glass of the French doors. Lightning lit up the scene. The destruction was complete.

But something else was visible in the eerie light. Nanny Jones was standing at the edge of the abyss, her arms folded, the mists swirling about her.

Mother screamed her name and although the wind was howling like 1,000 sirens, Nanny looked across the rose balcony at her and smiled. Then she vanished just as she had vanished years before.

—*Joyce Massuco, Seattle, Wash.*

My Father: My Guide

As a child I somehow became deeply religious and very early embraced the ideals of Christian life. When my father, Thomas DeVore, died on March 2, 1934, we were living in Huntington, West Virginia, where I had been born. I was only 11 when he died, the oldest of four children. My father's last words were, "Please take care of Maxine."

But I was haunted by a strange preoccupation. Had Dad himself become a Christian? If he had, his spirit lived. This was terribly important to me.

As it turned out, actual experience taught me Dad really was a Christian. He has been with me all through the years.

In late 1941, I married Herschell Ellis in Huntington and about the same time he was drafted into the Air Force, we learned that I was pregnant. Our son Gary Lee was born in November 1942, and almost immediately afterward my husband left Westover Field, Massachusetts, for overseas duty.

While carrying my baby I felt my father's presence for the first time. It was late October and I was sitting before the fireplace reading the Bible. I glanced up at the mantel to check the time and found Dad standing there, his back to the fire and one arm resting on the mantel. He smiled down at me and he looked peaceful and happy.

He told me to stop worrying about him. All was well, he said. He assured me that my marriage was a good one and that soon I would present him with a grandson. He also said my husband would come through the war although anxious times lay ahead. All Dad's prophecies came true.

About a week before my son's birth, I had a dream that remains as vivid today as if it had happened last night. I dreamed that Jesus stood between my husband and my father with His arms over their shoulders. My father was holding Gary Lee in his arms as they walked toward me down a grassy knoll. The full significance of this dream came to me eight months and 22 days later. I buried my son, Gary Lee, looking exactly as he did in that dream. And a few years later, cancer carried off my husband.

In September 1960, I married again, becoming Mrs. Charles T. McConnell. We made our home in San Bernardino and here in 1964 my father again came to me. He told me to get back to Mother as soon as possible. He did not say why, but by this time I had complete faith in my father's guidance. We decided to move to Michigan, thinking it would be easy to get work there and we would be relatively close to Mother who lived with my stepfather Elijah L. Coyle in Huntington, West Virginia.

About Christmas time, my stepfather suffered a severe heart attack and, after a six-week hospitalization, he died, leaving Mother alone. She wanted to stay in Huntington but now she too became ill and couldn't be left alone. After I found this house in Berkley, she joined me in November 1965. Since then I have seen Dad twice; once while Mother was in hospital in Royal Oak, Michigan, after heart attack and again early in 1966. Whenever trouble looms and I feel I don't know what I'm going to do, Dad comes. No one can tell me there is no survival after so-called death.

—*Maxine DeVore McConnell, Berkley, Mich.*

Do Guardian Angels Carry Spare Tires?

We joined the supply convoy late in the afternoon ready to move forward in support of the major offensive launched in late May 1945 against the strongly entrenched Japanese in the hills of southern Okinawa. In our three-quarter ton weapons carrier were Lt. Bob Mitchell, the popular and astute public relations officer of the 7th Infantry Division; W. Eugene Smith, one of the world's top photographers, then with Life magazine; Harold Smith, known affectionately as "Pack Rat Smith," famed war correspondent for the Chicago Tribune; Paige Abbott, the gallant brilliant photographer for INP; and myself, serving as staff correspondent for the Stars & Stripes.

The offensive did not move forward as planned and the convoy was stalled overnight along a stretch of some three miles. It was a night made memorable by parachute flares, machine gun tracers and heavy enemy mortar and artillery bombardment. By the next morning, the situation was "fluid." Our troops had advanced in some areas and in others the Japanese were counterattacking, tearing huge gaps in our lines.

Emergency orders to split up and disperse reached the convoy. We decided to make an attempt to get nearer the actual fighting, a necessity if we were to do our job—which was to get worthwhile news stories. We wound around a couple of the rugged Okinawan hills on a gravel road, which finally led into a small valley and on to a village. Over half the buildings in the town had been reduced to rubble. There seemed to be no activity in the vicinity, so a quick vote among the carrier's passengers demanded a stop for a bit of souvenir scrounging. We scattered like a covey of middle-aged females turned loose in a department store ahead of opening time on sale day.

We found some goodies here and there in the relatively undamaged houses near the edge of town but suddenly an explosion at the opposite end of the village brought our attention back to our position. Now mortar and artillery shells peppered the outskirts. Everyone made a mad dash to the weapons carrier with but one thought—retreat!

In a split second of stunned disbelief, we discovered the right rear tire of our vehicle was flat. Another salvo hit the far end of the village. To change the tire fast was imperative and we searched frantically for the tools. The jack was in the toolbox . . . but there was no spare tire!

The exploding shells were working their way closer. Harold Smith spotted three or four Japanese scurrying around in the wrecked buildings on the farthest outskirts of the village. It came to us that we were probably on the edge of a Japanese counterattack. For our defense we had one M–1 rifle, one carbine, and one .45 revolver.

Scanning the hills around us, we saw not one friendly GI, Marine, tank, or gun of any kind. We were on our own. Should we make a run for the nearest hill? Take cover in one of the village houses? Try to drive the carrier with a flat tire? It was a good 400 yards to the nearest hill and the terrain leading to it was open on all sides. To remain in the village would certainly mean a gunfight. And riding a crippled carrier on an open stretch of road would make us sitting ducks for the Japanese mortarmen.

At that moment, in one of the most exposed, dangerous, and insoluble situations any of us ever had faced, a most remarkable salvation came about nothing less than a miracle. Bob Mitchell and Gene Smith simultaneously recognized it. Some 30 feet ahead of the carrier in the ditch near the edge of the road lay a brand-new three-quarter ton weapons carrier tire, full of air, mounted on a wheel and ready to roll!

We had the carrier jacked up and the wheels switched in what had to be record time. The shelling continued spasmodically, punctuated by the popping sounds of Japanese rifles. But our good luck held. No shell fragments or bullets came near us while we piled into the carrier, made a tight U-turn, and roared back toward the area where we knew for certain the American lines still held firm.

To this day, a reasonable explanation of how that brand-new tire and wheel came to be lying in that precise spot at that precise time has not been advanced. The best knowledge we could develop was this: (1) no other three-quarter ton weapons carrier had been in the area previously; in fact, no other American vehicle of any type had been anywhere near there; (2) the tire could not possibly have fallen from our carrier, for it turned out that through some snafu our vehicle had no spare tire when drawn from the motor pool; (3) no major supply dumps had been established in the area; and (4) the Japanese were unlikely to have come into possession of such a tire and then abandoned it.

One thing we learned for sure: the village underwent a terrible bombardment and was overrun by Japanese troops within 15 minutes after we hot-rodded out of there.

—*Marshall K. McClelland, Chicago, Ill.*

Poltergeist Activity

Only the violent terror of the poltergeist ranks amongst the most feared of all the ghostly experiences presented in the pages of *FATE*. While most encounters with ghosts can be considered benign, the poltergeist represents the spectral aura of anger unleashed upon the world of the living. Its chaotic energy is on the rampage like a child's temper tantrum, destroying bits and pieces of homes or violently attacking the living, leaving grotesque scars. Whether this spectral rage is derived from some sort of frustration from being caught between two worlds or a demonic will whose only purpose is to inflict suffering, the poltergeist remains the frightening apex of ghostly encounters.

The poltergeist can become a part of an unsuspecting victim's life—attaching itself like a spectral parasite. Through a multitude of entries, the invading spirit becomes the bane of the unwitting person. People have purchased items at auctions and from antique stores only to discover they have brought home an unintended attachment. Others have moved into a new home or business only to be distressed as objects move on their own accord and whole rooms are turned asunder by seemingly invisible hands. The poltergeist appears in its most intrusive form in the possession of a living body, using it as the unwitting host for demonic creatures seeking to extend their reach into our dimension.

While no special effects–engorged film or tale of fiction has been able to capture the horror of those souls unfortunate enough to be plagued by such an entity, *FATE* has assembled a chapter of true tales from those who survived their experience to recount their stories.

Demonic Possession

Since the latter part of 1964, I have experienced strange happenings. They seemed to come to me in spells. At first they were widely separated, but as time passed they came more often. These strange experiences always came at night, generally as I was on the verge of sleep.

As my mind neared unconscious slumber and my whole body was relaxed, suddenly I would have a weird sensation, one that pulled my mind back to consciousness.

I would feel a surge of force, some physical yet invisible power crept over my body and seemed to press me down onto my bed. At first I thought it was a dream. But I actually couldn't move.

I strained my mind willing my body to move, but it was impossible. After a short time, the force slowly drained away. I felt as though I had emerged from a nightmare, but I knew it was more than that. After the first experience of this kind, I slept normally the rest of the night. In the morning I thought nothing of it, believing it due to overfatigue or something similar.

I had completely forgotten it when, perhaps a week later, it happened again. This time it was exactly the same, except that it was stronger. I seemed to lose contact with my surroundings. I could not sense physical contact with the bed. It was like swirling through dark space, aware only of my uncontrollable body, feeling nothing but my body itself. When it had passed, I was perspiring slightly from the ordeal. But with a prayer to God and the comfort of the small luminous cross over my bed, I again had no trouble falling asleep.

This phenomenon came back and each time with more power. I came to believe something alive and powerful and bad was trying to get into me—to enter my soul and my body. Each time it became more powerful and left me more afraid.

I lost track of how many times it happened. Maybe it was six times.

Then one night in January 1965, the phenomena occurred once more, only this time something else happened. The power increased, again leaving me control only over my mind. I trembled with fear when I heard sounds—a deep distant laughter, weird and unearthly. The laughter seemed to increase steadily in volume, together with the force. It was terrible. I heard the voice inside me! I felt the laughter invading my soul. It held an odd note of victory.

Then suddenly I knew! I knew this was a disciple of Satan, a demon from the Devil Himself. And I knew it was on the brink of possessing me.

I called out to God. I pleaded for my Savior's help. "Jesus, help me!"

The laughter stopped and the force dropped away, and I lay in a cold sweat that covered my body; but the warmth of peace covered my soul. God had answered my prayer and flooded my soul with faith and thanksgiving. The soft darkness was broken only by the glow of the small cross over my bed. I drifted off to sleep reassured with peace and the wonderful love of my Lord.

Now many weeks have passed and since January and I have been undisturbed.

—*Kenneth S. Leach, Cassopolis, Mich.*

The Pantry

In the summer of 1943, I lived in Los Angeles but spent frequent weekends visiting my sister, Margaret Wilson, who lived with her husband and four cats in the 1900 block of 43rd Street in San Diego.

Since both my sister and her husband worked, the cats often were alone with complete run of the house. Although their sandbox was in the rear, they spent much of their time in the living room, which occupied the full width of the front of the building.

Behind the living room was the bedroom, through which one had to pass in order to reach the combination dining room / kitchen. An eight-foot high partition separated the kitchen from a shelf-lined pantry along one side. Beyond the pantry another door led from the kitchen to the bath, and the kitchen range occupied a section of the partition wall between the two doors.

My custom, whenever I reached their home before they returned from work, was to put on a pot of coffee and then light the water heater. The cats would follow me from the moment I entered the front door.

One Saturday afternoon, I arrived an hour earlier than usual and sat down to drink a cup of coffee before lighting the water heater. All four cats had followed me into the kitchen and lay on the floor at my feet.

After a while, I rose and went to the pantry to light the water heater. But with my hand on the doorknob, I froze in absolute terror. There was something beyond that door! This knowledge was as real as the knowledge that I myself was standing in the kitchen.

I felt a furry body brush against my legs and heard a shrill screech as the four cats streaked past me into the bedroom with their hair on end. All four disappeared under the bed.

The back of my neck prickled and my solar plexus tensed with icy fear. I released the knob and stepped backward. After a few moments I regained enough composure to tell myself, *"Why, this is ridiculous! There is nothing, there!"*

Again I tried to open the door, but somehow I could not push it open. A force greater than any I ever had encountered held it shut from the other side.

Whatever was in the pantry had a powerful pervading reality, and I could sense that it was indescribably evil—the kind of evil no human mind ever can fathom.

Within a few minutes, I gave up and fled from the kitchen in panic, yanking the door shut behind me. I did not return until my sister came home.

Together we entered the pantry and lighted the water heater. Everything was as peaceful as always.

Even though I could not account for the cat's behavior, shame of my terror convinced me that my experience had been imagined. So I did not mention it.

Two years later, though, my sister surprised me by saying they had rented a house and were packing to move. The new house was much smaller and darker, more inconvenient and inaccessible from her work, and more expensive.

"Why on earth are you moving here?" I asked, puzzled at the suddenness of the shift.

"It's a little hard to explain," she said, "and I wouldn't tell anyone but you, but several times I have felt the presence of some malevolent thing in the pantry. I thought something was wrong with me until I realized the cats could feel it, and were scared out of their wits.

"Sometimes I couldn't go into the pantry—couldn't even open the door—and I'd have to wait for Bud to come home before I could start dinner.

"It's been getting worse lately, and I know whatever it is comes when we are not home, because the cats won't walk by the pantry door to get to their box. And you know how clean they've always been."

She was relieved to hear I had sensed this presence too, but neither of us could explain it. Nor has either one of us ever again felt the sheer power and cold wickedness of whatever was beyond that door.

—*Bonnie MacConnell, Tucson, Ariz.*

Ghost in the Mattress

When I was 10 years old, my father lost his job and we had to move to a large city where he planned to take a new job.

Having a large family, my mother took the first partially furnished house she could find. It seemed to be a nice place, being made of brick, with an open stairway, three rooms upstairs, and four more on the first floor.

The first night, my mother put all the children to sleep in one bedroom until she had a chance to clean up the other rooms.

An old mattress and cover, which had been left in one of the other bedrooms, was especially dirty and stained, and Mother was going to dispose of it.

I had not been asleep for long that night when I was awakened by something pulling at my throat and choking me. I was frightened to see the horrible face of an old man above me. His hands were clutching my throat. His head, arms, and shoulders seemed to come right out of a corner of a dirty, stained mattress.

I screamed and screamed, as I tried to pry his fingers from my throat.

My mother and father came running in to find me at the top of the stairs. Seeing that I was in a trance, they shook me to find out what had happened.

The drawstrings of my nightgown were tied tightly around my neck. I was near death. Beside me was the dirty old mattress that had been in another bedroom before I went to sleep.

The next day, my mother asked our neighbor about our home's former tenants.

She told us that an old man and his granddaughter had once lived there. One day the man went insane and choked his granddaughter to death. He then cut his own throat and died on the mattress, which had seemed to be the source of my horrible experience.

We did not spend another night that house.

—*Gertrude A. Paulsworth, Absecon, N.J.*

Iceland's Farm Poltergeist

In the north of Iceland there is a small farm called Saurar where Gudmundur Einarsson, a 72-year-old farmer, lives together with his wife, Margret Benediktsdottir, and their two grown children, a daughter called Sigurborg and a son called Benedikt.

On Wednesday, March 18, 1964, at 1:40 in the morning, Einarsson and his wife were waked by a sudden noise. They occupied separate beds, and between their beds, under the window, stood an oval table a little more than a yard in length, and weighing about 44 pounds. They noticed that this table had been moved away from the window and now was standing well out into the room. At first, they supposed this had been caused by an earthquake although, strangely enough, no other objects in the room had changed position.

The next afternoon, Mrs. Margret Benediktsdottir and her daughter, Sigurborg, were working outdoors when they heard a big crash from inside the house. No one was inside when they hurried in. There they saw that the kitchen table had been moved to the center of the floor and a pile of crockery, which had been placed top of it, now lay broken on the floor. Every now and then throughout the rest of that day, they noticed things being moved to and fro.

That night, Mr. Einarsson and his wife were awakened once more at 4:20 in the morning by the dining room table being moved.

Next day, March 19, a reporter from the newspaper Morgunblaoio, Mr. Thordur Jonsson, came for a visit, together with his chauffeur. He has said that, after having sat sometime in the lounge conversing with the farmer and his wife, they were invited into the kitchen for some coffee. The two old people went in first, the reporter followed and last came the chauffeur. No one remained behind in the lounge. As the chauffeur entered the kitchen, a noise was heard from the lounge. He immediately returned to the lounge, the others following him. There the table had been pushed a couple of yards across the floor.

That same day, another son of the elderly couple, Bjorgvin, turned up at Saurar farm for a few weeks stay.

Friday, March 20, at 2:30 p.m. the daughter was in the kitchen, her mother was speaking on the telephone in the lounge, and the father was outdoors with his two sons, when suddenly Sigurborg noticed that a big cupboard standing against the wall was beginning to move. She hastily caught a small wireless set, which had been placed on top of the cupboard, and, no sooner had she done so, than the cupboard crashed to the floor.

The next morning, March 21, at 9:30 a.m. the cupboard again fell flat on the floor. No one was in the kitchen at that time. The old woman was in the adjoining room with her son, Bjorgvin, when they heard the noise. The daughter had left home about an hour before this. She was going to stay with her sister at Reykjavik for a few weeks as she was beginning to suffer from nerves.

The news of this phenomena had by now reached the capital and the place was invaded by hordes of reporters and curious persons.

On Saturday, I traveled to Saurar on behalf of the Society for Psychical Research, together with some other members of the board. We stayed at the farm for three hours. The medium, Hafsteinn Biornsson, accompanied us. We did not witness any telekinetic phenomena, but we were shown the broken crockery and the cupboard in the kitchen, which had now been fastened to the wall. The farmer's wife told us that while the family was having lunch in the kitchen that same day the table at which they were seated suddenly began to move and they hurriedly put their hands on the crockery so that it would not fall on the floor.

We organized a séance with the medium, but it did not result in our discovering the causes of the mysterious phenomena.

After discussing the matter with the residents, I am convinced that none of them has deliberately caused the phenomena to occur.

One of the most eminent geologists of Iceland came to the farm and concluded after his research that the theory of an earthquake was out of the question. Later, another specialist turned up, bringing with him a seismograph, but he found no traces of an earthquake either.

The phenomena continued almost every day until April 3, the last week being the most eventful. The big table in the lounge was moved many times a day, even tipped over, and in the end it had to be tied to the wall. Then the top was broken off. Framed photographs fell down from the walls of the lounge together with other small objects: several of which were smashed.

Between the lounge and the kitchen is a small room in which the daughter slept before leaving for Reykjavik. In there, some objects began to move also. A small tray hanging on the wall was thrown across the room several times onto the divan where the girl had slept.

In the kitchen, objects were seen to move and in the pantry, which is fitted with shelves full of various things, plates from one of the shelves repeatedly were thrown to the floor where they broke into small pieces, while objects standing on the other shelves did not move at all.

On April 3, Mrs. Margret Benediktsdottir was taken to the hospital, about 30 miles away from the farm, on account of some illness. She remained there for eight days. In the meantime, the phenomena ceased completely. But two days after her return they began once more, although with much less frequency and vigor than before. A little later they totally ceased, and since then there has been no recurrence.

At the end of May, the American parapsychologist, Mr. W. G. Roll, Project Director of the Psychical Research Foundation in North Carolina, came to Iceland.

I accompanied him on two trips to Saurar for a further examination of the phenomena, which by then, unfortunately, had ceased to occur. We both concluded they must have belonged to the so-called "poltergeist" type of phenomena. We questioned the residents very thoroughly regarding the nature of the phenomena and were shown which objects had been moved and in what way. The main points we discovered were these:

1. Apparently the objects were moved chiefly from west to east, although some moved in other directions. It should be noted that the lines of direction crossed each other at a certain point on the kitchen floor.

2. The objects were moved, sometimes damaged or ruined, totally without regard to their ownership in each case.

3. The forces behind the phenomena did not seem to be endowed with intelligence. The moving objects did not appear to respond to anyone's thoughts or wishes, nor was there any kind of teasing connected with any particular person living at the farm.

On the other hand there are several indications that the phenomena may have been connected in some way with the old woman. The direction of movement of most of the objects pointed to the kitchen where she worked every day. She was the only person always present when the phenomena occurred. They ceased as soon as she left for the hospital and started again shortly after her return to the farm. They continued after the daughter left for Reykjavik and while the farmer and his son, Biorgvin,

were out fishing. They also occurred while the younger
son, Benedikt, was not at home but up in the mountains
tending the sheep.

—*Rev. Sveinn, Vikingur, Iceland*

Poltergeist Wrecks Business Office

The last place one would expect to find a poltergeist is in
a busy office building in a large industrial city like Oakland, California.

But on June 15, 1964, at about 2:15 p.m., I walked
into the office of court reporter George Wheeler at 1904
Franklin St., Oakland, and saw a poltergeist at work.
During the next three days, I was present while literally
dozens of inexplicable phenomena occurred.

George Wheeler's normally quiet office had become
the scene of a parade of policemen, reporters, photographers, television cameramen, and poltergeist experts, real
and phoney. For a time, Wheeler's work, taking down by
stenotype and transcribing the testimony of the Alameda
courts, came to an absolute standstill.

The story began for me shortly after 2:00 p.m., June
15. Roy Grimm, city editor of The Oakland Tribune,
gave me the Franklin Street address. "We had a police
call that things are jumping around over there," he said.

"What do you mean?" I asked.

"Poltergeist," he said and winked.

It didn't even sound like a story. Nevertheless, I
hopped into a cab and rode about seven blocks to the

Medical Building, in Oakland's downtown business district.

I took the elevator to the third floor and joined several persons milling around outside Wheeler's office. Almost immediately, we heard a loud crash from an empty room adjoining Wheeler's suite of three offices. The door was open and I looked in to see a metal cabinet lying on its back.

Feeling a little unnerved, I walked into Wheeler's office and introduced myself. I found that the normal occupants of the office were Wheeler himself, his wife Zolo who is also a court reporter, court reporters Robert Caya and Calvert Bowles, and two transcribers, Helen Rosenberg and John Orfanides.

George Wheeler was not present when I arrived, but Oakland police officer Charles Nye was there, having come to the office about 15 minutes earlier in response to a call.

Wheeler's office is a suite of three rooms, side by side and connected by doors, which usually stand open. Wheeler occupies the room on the far right, which also contains a small cupboard in which the staff keeps coffee-making equipment, wax for polishing desks and floors, and other miscellanea. I shall refer to this as the coffee cupboard.

The center room is the main entrance to the offices and is usually occupied by the transcribers, Mrs. Rosenberg and John Orfanides.

The room on the left contains several telephones, dictaphone equipment, a water cooler, wall cabinets for storing papers and equipment, and a movable counter filled with office supplies.

Mrs. Wheeler took me immediately to her husband's room, which was a mess. An ashtray lay on the floor, broken. Outside the door of the coffee cupboard was a pile of smashed crockery lying in a pool of water.

Officer Nye told me that he had inspected the premises as soon as he arrived. He said he entered the coffee cupboard and observed an empty blue flower vase and a large glass water pitcher of the type commonly used in hotels, sitting near the edge of a shelf.

"I thought these objects might be dislodged if there was any vibration in the building, so I pushed them right back against the wall," he said. The shelf is about 18 inches deep.

A few minutes later, while Officer Nye was in another room, and Wheeler's room was apparently vacant, the pitcher and vase flew through the air, made a right turn, and shattered on the floor of the office, beside Wheeler's desk.

While Officer Nye was telling me this, there was a banging sound from the room on the left. One of the telephones had fallen to the floor. I hastily called the office and asked them to send a photographer.

Jim Edelen, a veteran of the Tribune staff, arrived a few minutes later. He asked John Orfanides to pose with the shattered objects outside the coffee cupboard. Edelen took his picture and the two turned to leave the room. As they went out the door, there was a crash behind them. They turned to find the debris on the floor now covered with white powder. A large jar of Coffee-Mate powdered cream substitute had flown out of the coffee cupboard and smashed on the floor.

Mrs. Rosenberg, who does most of her work in the office, was present during more of the manifestations than anyone else. She told me the first unusual occurrence had taken place about two weeks previously. At that time, the telephones began acting up. The row of lights along each telephone would light up in quick succession, but there would be nobody on the line.

The telephone company could find nothing wrong with the instruments, but when the trouble persisted, they changed the phones.

The electric typewriters were next to go. These typewriters all have small coil springs underneath each key so they return to the original position after they have been depressed. It is necessary to take the top off the machine to get at them.

Inexplicably, the electric typewriters in Wheeler's office began going haywire. The springs went limp, twisted together and balled up. Repairmen came and took them away, leaving loan machines in their place. The springs on the loan machines promptly did the same thing, leaving the recorders helpless to do any typing. When the original machines were returned, their springs began acting up again.

"Those springs normally last for the life of the machine," Bob Goosey, a sales representative for the typewriter company, told me.

"We haven't replaced three of those springs in the past 10 years. But during the last few days we've replaced about 100 in Wheeler's machine. We've practically exhausted our stock of springs."

While I was in Wheeler's office on June 15, all eight of the phones kept sliding off the desks and falling to the floor with monotonous regularity. We got tired just picking them up. The metal top of a typewriter flew across the room and struck a wall, leaving a dent. A metal postal scale sailed across the room. A porcelain cup sitting on Mrs. Wheeler's desk jumped 12 feet into the air and shattered against the ceiling, leaving a brown stain.

Abruptly, about 4:00 p.m., the phenomena stopped.

During the night, George Wheeler moved a desk and some of his equipment into an empty office downstairs in an attempt to get away from the rampaging poltergeist. The desk was taken from the left office and the phones from it were placed on the floor.

When I arrived the next morning, Bob Caya was in the abandoned room talking on the telephone and looking out the window. I heard a thud and entered the room instantly. Caya's back was to the door and he was still talking. On the floor was a dictaphone pedal which apparently had flown out of a cabinet and struck the counter. There was a mark on the counter.

I began to keep a log of the poltergeist phenomena. Every time something happened, I made a notation describing it and the time it occurred. I did this for only one hour, between 10:30 and 11:30 a.m., June 16, but there were no fewer than 12 entries in it. An interesting thing this log reveals is that the entries are all exactly five minutes apart. In other words, something happened every five minutes.

One of the first things I noticed on entering Wheeler's room on this second day was a metal box full of papers on the floor. It apparently had fallen there soon after the office opened. I picked it up, examined it, and placed it on a metal filing cabinet. Later, while I stood in the doorway of the room with my back to it, the box flew about eight feet and hit the floor with a frightening crash. I whirled around. There was no one in the room.

A door, which had been taken off the entrance to the adjoining vacant office, had been left standing against the wall at about a 30 degree angle. It pitched forward with a bang—causing everybody to jump.

Also, it soon became evident that the poltergeist had followed the hapless staff to the office downstairs on the second floor. From there a typewriter top flew off and sailed out a window, striking the roof of a parked car on the street.

By this time, the eerie happenings had been well publicized and all kinds of people kept popping in either to watch for poltergeists or to take some part in the proceedings. One of the strangest of these was an occultist from San Francisco who began burning incense in little brass jars and staring soulfully at the ceiling.

The most important visitor was Dr. Arthur Hastings, of Stanford University. Dr. Hastings teaches speech and drama, but he long has been a devout student of abnormal occurrences and has worked with Duke University's famed Institute of Parapsychology.

After carefully weighing the evidence and talking to all the witnesses, including myself, Dr. Hastings ventured the opinion that this was "a genuine poltergeist phenomenon."

Since he is an accomplished magician himself, Dr. Hastings was able to discount the use of magic in many of the phenomena observed. One of the things that helped convince him was my obliging metal box. He telephoned Duke that night and was asked to continue his investigations on their behalf.

The poltergeist continued to be active sporadically during the afternoon of my second day. A typewriter was tossed from a table in an empty room on the second floor. A large electric coffee percolator fell to the floor, cups exploded, telephones crashed, and a filing cabinet toppled over.

The filing cabinet, which was made of wood, was one of the few things that any of us actually saw moving. Usually the objects would fly while the room was empty or while its occupants were looking the other way. But Bob Goosey, the typewriter man, was standing in a doorway when the cabinet suddenly turned sideways and fell over right before his eyes.

On Wednesday morning, June 17, the phenomenon reached a thunderous climax. Early in the morning, Cal Bowles and John Orfanides opened the office. In quick succession the water cooler toppled over, soaking the left office and covering the floor with broken glass; an eight-foot high wooden cabinet containing office supplies came crashing down in the center room, scattering papers in every direction; and the movable counter in the left room toppled over onto its back.

I arrived after all this took place and discovered that the police had taken John Orfanides down to headquarters for questioning. The poltergeist activity, meanwhile, had stopped.

Orfanides later was released and he went home. The Wheeler office, now a shambles, was quiet.

This lasted for several more days, and I began to feel confident that the poltergeist had given up. Dr. Hastings told me this is frequently the case. The phenomenon will reach a climax and seemingly burn itself out.

Then, 12 days later, on June 29, there was a stunning development! I had spent the afternoon on an assignment in San Francisco. When I returned to the office, I was told that John Orfanides again had been taken down to police headquarters and had confessed to throwing the objects around. He held them behind his back, he said, and flipped them when no one was looking. He bent the typewriter springs by inserting a bent paper clip and rak-ing them.

This hardly explained the other occurrences, but the police were satisfied. They asked John if he would talk to the press. John asked first if he could talk only to me. But the officers told him they thought it would be better if he saw all of the reporters and television men at once. They scheduled a full-blown press conference and since I was on the other side of San Francisco Bay, another reporter attended as representative from our newspaper.

At the conference, the police outlined John's admis-sions. John glumly agreed and the story went out on tele-vision and in the San Francisco newspapers that John had confessed all and the case was now closed. This was picked up by the wire services in San Francisco and the story was flashed across the nation within hours that the Oakland poltergeist was just an admitted prankster.

John's confession shocked me. In fact, I didn't believe a word of it. This was not because I had become particularly friendly with John or because I was unwilling to believe that he was a prankster. It was for the sole rea-son that John had been at my side or directly within my line of vision when poltergeist activity was taking place two rooms away or on another floor. It was because on innumerable occasions I had been the first person into the room when objects flew, within a second or two of hearing a sound, and had found the rooms empty. I sim-ply did not believe that John could have fooled me so completely.

Although I was too late for the press conference, I started immediately for the apartment where John lives, taking a photographer as a witness. John had not arrived home, but his sporty red Thunderbird rolled up just as we were about to give up.

I slid into the front seat beside John, and Leo Cohen, the photographer, got into the back.

"Why did you make this confession John?" I asked.

"Because, as far as the police are concerned, it's all over," he said.

"John, I know and you know that you couldn't have thrown those things around," I said. "Isn't that true?"

"Of course, it's true," he said.

John readily repudiated his confession, leaving us with the question as to why he had made it in the first place. It certainly wasn't for publicity or any hope of personal gain. In fact, he now might expect that Wheeler would fire him for wrecking the office.

John Orfanides is an intelligent, hard-working young man. He is only 20 years old; he is newly married and responsible. He has had little or no experience with the police and he is emotionally high-strung. He was born in Pennsylvania but spent several years in high school in California's Napa County.

He was extremely upset when the police talked to him. He wanted to get off the interrogation griddle, as quickly and painlessly as he could. He told me that the police kept suggesting ways he could have made the objects move, reminding him at the same time that he probably would not be prosecuted.

"Finally I began to agree with the methods they suggested," he said. "I told them I threw everything because that was the only way I thought it could have been done.

"But these things are just as much a mystery to me as to everybody else."

This is the way matters stand now. John is doing his work at home and the poltergeist activity has stopped.

But even though John Orfanides is innocent of any wrongdoing, there is still a possibility that he might be the agent who caused the strange manifestations.

Dr. Hastings already had explained that, in the classic poltergeist formula, there is usually a young person, often just passing the age of puberty, who is always present when the events take place. They are not aware of it and are just as startled and frightened as everyone else. They don't do anything physically. The phenomena just occur in their presence. John is a little old to fall into this category, but he was the youngest person in the office and when he wasn't there the phenomena had stopped.

John has agreed to cooperate fully with Dr. Hastings and any other experts Dr. Hastings may wish to consult. Perhaps they may come up with some answers to a phenomenon which is really not so rare, but which is contrary to the known laws of physics. Most persons just won't believe it can happen. I didn't until I walked into George Wheeler's office and saw it for myself.

—*Jim Hazelwood, FATE contributing writer*

The Ghost that Moved to Our House

In February 1917, my parents, Pat and Leina Murphy, were faced with the financial problems that often beset newlyweds. Because rent was the largest single expenditure, they and two other couples, also recently married, decided to pool their resources and share a place to live.

The friends house-hunted for weeks without finding a house with the necessary requirements of one bedroom for each couple. At last one was located on the outskirts of Santa Ana, California. This house had seven bedrooms and rented for an absurdly small sum. Situated at the end of a long drive, in a farming area in the small community of Tustin on Pacific Street, the great house was surrounded by immense Magnolia trees. Three stories high, it glistened white in the sunlight. The couples moved in, piling boxes of dishes and a trailer load of belongings on the first floor while they eagerly set out to explore their new home. Claude and Catherine Nelson settled for a front view bedroom. Dick and Nora Chapman took a large, airy room next to the stairs after tossing a coin with my parents, who then took a bedroom at the end of the long hall. Since the house was so large, it was decided to close off the third story to conserve heat and simplify housekeeping. Settling took very little time for none of the couples had much furniture. And luckily the house had been rented fully furnished.

The interior of the house and the spacious gardens, terraced and flagstoned, bespoke the wealth of the owners.

The young people wondered why anyone would choose to leave such a lovely home. Mother, an avid student and collector of antiques, was overwhelmed at the treasures the house contained. Across the front room, curved into a semicircle, was a great tile fireplace. This room was a complete oval. The ceiling was domed, with pink and white cherubs winging their way toward its center. The small colonnades around the walls matched, in miniature, the immense columns supporting the outer porch. All in all, it was a lovely house.

Shortly after they moved in, Nora Chapman, Kate Nelson, and Mother were polishing the heavy paned doors, which separated the front room from the small hallway leading to the stairs. The stairs were circular, twisting in a delicate, beautiful arch. Suddenly, all three girls heard the sound of someone running. They turned in unison. The full length of the stairway was in sight. Yet, despite the sound of footsteps, the stairs were empty. Discussion that night at the dinner table brought smiles from the men and the matter was dismissed.

Several nights later, the household was awakened by Kate screaming, "Something is trying to smother me. I can't get up."

They rushed into her bedroom to find her fighting some invisible force, flailing wildly with her hands. Her husband was ashen-faced with fear, and trying to push Kate out of bed. Abruptly, Kate was thrown onto the floor with such force that her ankle twisted sickeningly under her and her head hit the wall. Claude and Kate wanted to leave the house that very night but were persuaded against doing so.

The doctor who was called to tend Kate's injured ankle was from one of the area's first families and acquainted with the owners of the house. When told the details of the night he murmured cryptically, "Little wonder, considering this house." Then he refused to say another word.

Some days later, the footsteps again were heard running up the stairs. This time they paused on the landing, then continued to the top of the stairway. The bathroom door was heard to swing open and slam shut. Water was heard to turn on in the washbowl. My father went up the stairs and into the bathroom. It was empty, but the water was running full tilt in the bowl. Father turned it off and went back downstairs. Later that same day, the footsteps again went up the stairs. This time Father ran after them. Again they paused on the landing, then continued toward the bathroom. Father, unbelieving, heard the sound of the door opening and slamming, although the door itself never moved. The sound of water running into both the washbowl and bathtub became clearly audible. But this time the water was not actually running.

Shortly after this, when the entire family sat at the dinner table, they heard the sound of footsteps running heavily down the stairs.

Everyone rushed into the front hall. Silently, the huge sliding doors of the front room slid open. A brisk, cold breeze blew past. Later that same night, as Claude made certain the doors were locked, he commented, "It's more likely that we're locking up to protect what is on the outside from what we've got inside."

Claude came up the stairs and heavy footfalls began a descent. Invisible, they passed Claude on the landing. At first he felt a cold breath of air. This was followed by a nauseating odor, an incredibly foul, acrid stench that hung about the stairway for days.

The couples would have moved but, of course, the rent could not be bettered. Following their decision to stay on, a new manifestation occurred. In the darkness, before the first glimmer of dawn, they waked to hear the sound of a heavy wagon laboring down the drive. Clearly they heard the clatter of horses' hooves, the clip-clop of shod feet intermingled with the jingling of the harness. Continuing around the circle drive toward the rear of the house, the wagon noise stopped. Then came the sound of men's voices, first the murmur of conversation, then the elevated pitch indicative of an argument. No words were distinguishable. A new sound began. Obviously, heavy timbers were being hoisted off the wagon and dropped heavily onto the ground. Just as the sun's first rays became visible, the creaking wagon, carrying the voices, lumbered off into the distance.

At least twice each week thereafter this occurred.

Several weeks passed and a new disturbance took place. At the rear of the house stood an old windmill, rusty and unused. Here, again before dawn, clanking noises began at the top of the windmill. Then came the sound of a falling body. Whatever was falling, invisibly, hit the windmill's structure on the way down and came to rest with a heavy "plop" on the ground.

Father mentioned this odd occurrence in town one day and was told that some years before, a hired man had fallen to his death from atop the windmill when a sudden gust of wind had caught its fans, breaking them loose from the stabilizing brake.

Time passed, with the couples trying to adjust to the many and varied noises associated with the house.

An entirely new experience occurred one morning. Dick had gone into the basement for a jar of fruit. Standing on a small box to reach the highest shelf, he suddenly felt a violent rocking motion. Thinking this was a typical California earthquake, he braced himself for the aftershock. The rocking motion increased, finally knocking Dick to the floor. The rolling motion stopped. From a corner of the dark room came a deep sigh, as though air was being expelled from a giant bellows. Another sigh ended abruptly. Clutching the jar of fruit, Dick reached the steps leading to the kitchen. As he reached the door, he again heard the sighing noises, sounding louder and louder, in great exhalations. The noise was cut off by his slamming the door. My father and Claude accused Dick of an attack of nerves. They both went down into the basement. Again, obligingly, came the huge, prolonged sighing. During their somewhat rapid ascent of the stairs the great sighing noise continued, stopping only when the kitchen door slammed behind him.

That day Claude went into town and purchased a large bolt, which he set into the basement door with huge screws. Mother, only half in humor, suggested they had a Minotaur in their basement. No one laughed.

One afternoon, Mother, Kate, and Nora went up the stairs leading to the third floor. In the distance, there was a large fire and the third-floor portico offered a fine view. They left the tall French doors open wide as they went out onto the porch. When the fire was out and the excitement over, Mother and her friends turned to find the doors shut. They could not force them open. Hours later, as darkness approached, their husbands returned home from work and rescued them. Inspection revealed that the bolt had been slipped into place and further secured by pressing it into the lower notch designed to prevent its sliding out again.

Shortly after this last occurrence, Mother's grandmother and grandfather, Mr. and Mrs. Clossen Woodruff, of San Bernardino, California, came for a visit. Great-Grandmother was a tiny woman whose frailty concealed a will of iron. She came from a large family all of whom were psychic. However, Great-Grandfather's religion taught that such things were "in league with the devil." Nevertheless, Great-Grandmother's aid was always sought in times of drought. Quietly, she would sit beside a pond of water, however small, and "concentrate on rain." It always rained shortly thereafter. She could command "with will power" a chair or any inanimate object to dance its way around the room. Her mother had been able to do this before her. One day Great-Grandfather came into the house in time to see his wife making a chair to hop around the room while their son, who weighed 205 pounds, sat upon it. Great-Grandfather's roars of anger were quieted only by Great-Grandmother's promise to drop all such activities.

Once inside Mother's home with its strange atmosphere, however, her promise fell by the wayside. As the family sat in the lovely front room before the tiled fireplace with its roaring fire, Great-Grandmother announced, "There are people here in the room with us."

Over the fireplace hung the large portrait of a blonde woman. Her face had delicate planes and exquisite coloring. Her hair fell over one shoulder in an attractive fashion. Her blue gown and pale yellow shawl were painted in intricate detail, by an obviously competent painter. Pointing to this portrait, Great-Grandmother said, "I get the distinct impression that woman died in one of the upstairs bedrooms. It was not a natural death, although everyone thought so. She died slowly, through poison."

A brief, warning look from Great-Grandfather brought the subject to an end.

The next morning, Mother, who was intrigued by psychic phenomena, pleaded with Great-Grandmother to attempt further "impressions." Great-Grandfather had gone to town and Nora and Kate were gone for the day also. Great-Grandmother said she would try once more but she wished to be alone in the room with the doors shut. Mother sat outside in the hall, at first hearing nothing.

Then came a loud rustling noise, like dry corn leaves in the wind. This noise became many voices rising and falling in tempo. Mother became alarmed and threw open the great sliding doors. Inside the room the heavy murmur of demanding voices continued. The air was bristling and electric. Great-Grandmother sat in a chair, obviously in trance. Mother was rubbing Great-Grandmother's wrists when Father and Great-Grandfather entered the room. They took Great-Grandmother to an upstairs room where Mother sat beside her while she rested.

Great-Grandmother, seeing that her husband had left the room, said, "I wish you had waited. 'They' were just ready to tell me what they wanted when you came in. A great tragedy took place here. Not only because the blonde woman died, but there is something inhuman here. I'm not easily frightened but, whatever it is, I am terrified."

Mother noticed that Great-Grandmother's face was unusually pale. Never before had Mother seen her afraid.

Next morning, Great-Grandfather began packing to leave for home. He had found the odd noises of the night annoying and had slept little. Great-Grandmother had stepped into the front room for one last glimpse of the portrait. Mother was in the kitchen brewing hot tea. Great-Grandmother's screams brought her rushing into the room. Only Great-Grandfather and Mother were at home that morning and she called out to him as she ran to help her grandmother. The small figure of Great-Grandmother lay on the floor. Her body tossed wildly from side to side in a struggle with some invisible foe. She pulled at her throat with both hands, managing another feeble cry for help. Finally, she rose from the floor and staggered over to the couch. Great-Grandfather dashed in to find Mother and Great-Grandmother both fighting an unseen force. By this time Great-Grandmother's face was blue. Clearly, the invisible foe was choking her to death.

Suddenly Great-Grandmother stood erect. She managed one heavy, tortured breath before the invisible fingers tightened on her throat once more. Terrified, Great-Grandfather began praying aloud, "In the name of God, let her go." Over and over he prayed these words. As quickly as it had begun, the onslaught stopped, using its remaining strength to slam Great-Grandmother to the floor. Great-Grandfather swept his wife into his arms, hurrying her to the car. "We'll never come back into this evil house again. I advise you to move at once, before some awful thing happens here."

As Mother kissed her grandmother goodbye she whispered, "I was 'talking' with the blonde woman when I saw this awful creature standing behind her. It was as big as a man, but like nothing I've ever seen before. It had orange hair, standing out from its head, stiff and wiry. Its hands curved into talons. The arms were like a man's, but covered with orange hair. It walked straight around the woman, put its face against mine and muttered, 'I'm going to kill you.' Look at my neck where its nails cut into my flesh. I want you to promise me you'll leave this house—

that you'll move right away. I know that this house will burn down within a short time. Nothing will be left but the foundation."

Until the day she died, Great-Grandmother carried small scars on her neck. And after her experience with "the monster" she was able to speak only in a raspy whisper.

The saga of the strange house ended quite suddenly one night. Kate and Claude had gone to their bedroom. Kate, as usual, had brushed her hair and then gotten into bed. With a startled shriek of agony, she began clawing at the bedclothes. Dick and Father rushed into the room to find Claude beating the bedclothes with his heavy shoe. Dad threw back the bed quilts to reveal, clamped onto Kate's foot, the largest black bat any of them ever had seen. Dad pried it loose while Dick knocked it to the floor with his shoe. Rising from the floor the bat circled the room, beating its wings against the window until a pane broke, and it swept out into the darkness.

The next morning, they agreed to move at once. The three couples separated to go their own ways. The house, with its exquisite furnishings, was left vacant. The owners apparently had adored moss roses. Each room had moss roses integrated into the decor. The lovely fragile china in the tall, glass-front cupboards was decorated with moss roses. Mother took away with her a porcelain chamber pot, tall and white, with the inevitable moss rose decoration. From the extensive library she took a small leather-bound edition of Lowell. These alone, of all the lovely things, exist today for, within a few weeks after they left, the house burned to the ground. Nothing was saved and nothing remained, except the foundations.

There is a sequel to this story, I am sorry to say.

The years following Great-Grandmother's death were uneventful. Occasional references to "the day Granny met the monster" were made by Uncle Jim. At that time, we all were living in Granny's old ranch house in San Bernardino. It had been built during the 1880s by Great-Grandfather. It was a warm, friendly house full of loving memories and of the treasures Granny had collected during her 60 years of marriage.

It was about 10 years after Great-Grandmother's death that Uncle Jim dashed downstairs, white-faced. He gasped, "You know that small door leading into the storage room? Believe it or not, I saw an orange-haired 'thing' poke its head out and then shut the door."

We laughed, "Come, now. You've imagined it!"

Uncle Jim shook his head. At various times after this, Uncle Jim complained of "something" in his room. Each time he was met with gales of derisive laughter.

Then Uncle Jim died.

Various members of the family spent their vacations in the old house. In 1948, my mother and father spent several weeks on the old ranch, taking along my son Mike, who was nine at that time. Of the three upstairs bedrooms, Mother and Mike occupied the center one which led onto an upstairs porch.

Father took the connecting room.

Mother rested comfortably the first night until around 3:00 a.m. when she awoke with a feeling that "someone" was in the room. Looking toward the veranda doorway she saw the outline of a man. She called out, thinking it was Dad, who suffered from insomnia. Steadily, the figure shuffled toward the bed and reaching it, peered down into her face. Mother said the face was unlike anything human.

Extending one arm, it pointed its grotesque hand toward Mike, who still slept peacefully. Reaching over the bed, across Mother, the creature jabbed a finger at Mike. Too terrified to make a sound, Mother tried to get out of bed. The creature backed away. Looking it full in the face, Mother saw a grinning mouth with huge, yellow teeth. Its eyes were almost hidden in a series of mottled lumps. Darting its slitted eyes toward Mike it again tried to approach the bed. Mother planted herself in its path. Brushing her aside it lunged toward Mike, who was wide-awake. Mother grabbed a handful of thick long hair with one band and desperately clutched a hairy, scaly arm with the other. In the moonlight which shown through the window, she saw huge hands which curved into long talons, reach again for Mike. Mike sat upright in bed, screaming in terror, while Mother wrestled with her weird assailant. Using her fists, she hit the bloated face. Clinging to the wiry hair, pushing it away from the side of the bed, she screamed for Dad.

Aiming a blow at Mother's head the creature tried a new tack. Veering around to the end of the bed it reached toward Mike from there. Mother jumped into the middle of the bed to face it again. In its eagerness to reach Mike, it began tugging the bedclothes, pulling them toward the foot of the bed, dragging Mother and Mike along. Grabbing the hair of its head, Mother hit it again in the stomach. Mike, almost out of his mind with fear, shrieked, "Grandpa, Grandpa, come quick."

Dad switched on his light and rushed into the room. Blinded momentarily, he did not see the figure leave the side of the bed. It backed toward the open door of the upper porch. Mother, reassured by Dad's presence, followed. Turning to look her full in the face, it again pointed toward Mike. In the light from Dad's room Mother could see it wore clothing of some kind. A light-colored, tight-fitting, one-piece suit of a thin material that ended at knees and elbows. The projecting limbs were covered with long, thick hair. Orange hair stuck out wildly in all directions from its head. Thick, bulbous lips drew back over crooked, yellow teeth. Bristly orange hair protruded from its nose, which was flattened and grossly misshapen. Taking a step toward Mother it gestured animatedly in Mike's direction. Then turning, it shuffled through the doorway.

Dad peered down the expanse of porch. Over 20 feet above the yard, this porch had no entrance except through the upstairs bedroom. But nothing was visible. However a fetid odor as of decaying flesh permeated the bedroom.

After this incident, no member of the family except Dad dared sleep in the upstairs bedrooms. He was determined to wait the return of the unknown visitor. A slight, sickening odor of decay continued to hang in the air.

Eventually, about 1952, the house was sold to the Riverside Water Company and razed. To our family, at least, it seems possible that creatures haunting one house can, if they choose, move their operations to another.

During Great-Grandmother's encounter with the creature calculated physical harm was done. But, although it had ample opportunity to seriously harm Mother, it seemed intent only on reaching my son Mike. We wonder what would have happened if it had reached Mike.

From what environs it originated, to what regions it returned, we can merely speculate. But we are in unanimous agreement that further visitations would be unwelcome.

—M. G. *Murphy, FATE contributing writer*

Two Midwest Poltergeists

In Jackson, Michigan

Modern American poltergeists, like other modern Americans, seem to be enjoying much longer lives than their pioneering ancestors. The Victor Lincoln family of Jackson, Michigan, believes they have one that is now in its third year of activity.

For more than two years, the Lincoln family thought they were the target of malicious prowlers. Frequently, on returning home to an empty house, they found lamps overturned, bottles and light bulbs strewn about, water running, and doors that had been shut tight, were now open.

When Jackson police failed to turn up anything, the Lincolns put double locks on their doors, but still they occasionally found their house had been partially vandalized.

Since last October 30, the Lincolns have been convinced that the intruders are not the type police can do anything about.

In Vic Lincoln's own words, the house is "spooked."

Dishes and bottles suddenly hurtle through a room, moans come from the basement, heavy footsteps sound throughout the house, doors swing open by themselves, water and gas jets turn on for no explainable reason, and books transport themselves from bookcases to chairs and beds, he reports.

In a word, the Lincolns believe they have a poltergeist. Except for the long span of the activity, the Lincolns would have an almost perfect case history, an absolute parallel to a dozen previously documented reports.

However, the report of phenomena occurring over more than two years is very unusual. Dr. Nandor Fodor, noted psychoanalyst has had this to say about the "life" of a poltergeist: "The lifetime of a poltergeist is always limited. The aggressive energies that manifest themselves are spent in a few weeks—or in two to three months at best—and quiet returns to the house where everything went bump before."

The stretch-out of activity at the Lincoln home already has attracted two experienced researchers from the privately endowed Psychical Research Foundation of Durham, North Carolina. The researchers are Dr. William G. Roll, project director of the Psychical Research Foundation, and his associate, Dr. John Freeman. Dr. Roll spent four days in the house, living with the Lincoln family, in December and returned for a weeklong visit late in January. Dr. Freeman spent three days there in December.

A complete report of their findings is expected at a later date, but they did leave Mrs. Beatrice Lincoln with the impression that they believe "someone's memory has impregnated itself in the house."

"I don't know exactly what it means, but from my talks with the doctor, I gather that he believes that somehow the memories of a former resident of the house have remained here after the resident's death," she said.

The "former resident" is likely to have been a member of the Lincoln family, since the home has been occupied by several generations of this family since 1912. The house is now for sale and some observers wonder if the poltergeist might be protesting the impending loss of his family, since the phenomena are reported to have intensified after the house was put up for sale.

The present generation living in the house consists of the senior Lincolns and the three youngest of their six children. These include two sons, 15 and 22, and a daughter, Georgine, 13. It is evident that the household does not lack for the teenagers often considered to be central figures in poltergeist phenomena.

At 13, Georgine is exactly the same age as Linda Beck, of the Indianapolis family currently having poltergeist problems.

Victor Lincoln is a machinist, and the oldest son, John, is now looking for employment. He was discharged from the Army last August and has been living at home since then.

On the night of October 30, John and his mother were seated in the living room reading.

Suddenly they heard a noise, as though a very heavy person was walking up the basement steps, which lead both to the kitchen and to a bedroom occupied by John and his brother Thomas, 15.

"The footsteps stopped, but all at once we heard a sound as though someone was pounding terrifically hard on a door, and Thomas came running from his bedroom shouting that someone was trying to break in," Mrs. Lincoln recalls.

By now, Vic Lincoln was up and had his shotgun. With the dog, Jackson, he opened the basement door and went into the cellar.

"As soon as I opened the door, the pounding stopped and there was nothing there. I didn't notice anything peculiar in the cellar, but apparently Jackson did. His hair went up on end and he wheeled around and bounded up the stairs, whining all the while," Vic says.

From that day on, the Lincoln's have known little peace.

"We've gotten so used to hearing steps and moans everywhere at any time that we are learning to live with them. But we still can't take these bottles whizzing through the house for no apparent reason, breaking windows and dishes," Lincoln says.

Thus far no one has been injured seriously, but Mrs. Lincoln was nicked in the leg by a flying paring knife that she says had been in a drawer in the kitchen. At the time, Mrs. Lincoln was the only one in the house and she was lying on a couch in the living room, which is separated from the kitchen by a dining room.

Last Christmas was particularly harrowing for the Lincolns.

Mrs. Lincoln reveals that the family had their Christmas tree for only two days during the holidays.

"Christmas Eve, the entire family was in the living room when the lights suddenly flew off the tree and scattered about the house. That was enough for us, and the tree came down," she says.

Harry Kellar, a Jackson County probation officer who was not previously acquainted with the Lincolns, visited them after he heard about strange doings in the house. He says, "Everyone was sitting in the front room talking when Mr. Lincoln said he heard water running. We went into the bathroom and water was pouring from a tap.

"A little later, while we were back in the front room, someone smelled gas and we discovered that the gas jets on the stove had been opened, although there was no flame."

Kellar recalls that he went to the Lincoln house a skeptic and admits he's still not certain that there is no reasonable explanation of what happened.

"But I do know this. I was keeping track of everyone, and we were all in the living room when the water went on and the gas jets opened," he says.

Mr. and Mrs. Clarence Gingras, friends of both the Lincoln's and Mr. Kellar, recall water and gas were mysteriously turned on while they were in the house in December.

On another occasion, they were at the Lincoln's waiting for Kellar to join them there.

"My husband had just talked to Harry and he said it would be about 15 minutes before he would get over. About five minutes later, while my husband and I were seated in the living room couch and all the Lincolns were in the room with us, we heard footsteps on the porch.

"We both heard the steps at the same instant because we each turned to the other and remarked that Harry had arrived sooner than we had expected.

"But when Vic and my husband went to the door there was no one there. And though the porch was covered with new snow, there were no footprints. Both my husband and I are positive we heard footsteps on that porch and we heard them at the same instant," Mrs. Gingras says with conviction.

When Kellar arrived a short time later, footprints in the snow marked his path across the porch.

Despite these presumably impartial observations, there are many in Jackson who insist that the Lincolns' "haunted house" is either a hoax or that the family has been, collectively victimized by overworked imaginations.

I have spent approximately 10 hours in the Lincoln house on three separate occasions. On two occasions, both during daylight hours, nothing happened. But during an evening visit, lasting from about 7:30 p.m. to shortly after midnight, a number of things did occur.

There were four of us, including a young woman, along with the Lincolns and four of their children in the house that night.

In the first hour, nothing happened as we sat around the dining and living rooms, talking and watching television.

Suddenly, though, Mr. Lincoln said he heard water running. Everyone immediately dashed into the bathroom where water was running, in fact, pouring from a tap. It is certain that everyone in the house was in either the dining or living rooms when the water turned on.

Sometime later, while all were in the living room, someone reported they smelled oil. Again everyone made a mad dash, this time to a rear bedroom where, indeed, a strong odor of oil was coming from a space heater.

I had been in that room a short time before and, out of curiosity, had checked the heater. It was not on. There was no odor. I am reasonably sure no one had entered the room between the time I checked the burner and we all rushed back to check on the oil odor.

After this had been investigated (the odor disappeared shortly after we all crowded into the bedroom) and we were moving back toward the living room, something smashed against a metal closet in the bedroom. This turned out to be a small glass bottle, which was found on the floor beside the closet.

While we were examining the bottle, the lights in the house went out. They came back on when Mr. Lincoln replaced a fuse in the basement box.

Were unnatural forces responsible for these occurrences? Perhaps.

But I recall that several years ago, while living in an apartment in a rather old building, I was plagued with a bathroom tap that kept turning on by itself. A defective tap, rather than an unnatural force turned out to be the culprit on that occasion.

In any evaluation of what occurred while I was in the Lincoln's house, a number of things should be kept in mind.

Each time something happened, except when the lights went out which was apparent to everyone simultaneously, it was the Lincolns who first reported that something was going on.

And each time they gave the report there was a great deal of commotion with everyone, the Lincolns in the lead, rushing to investigate. With the rushing to and fro, the milling about, and the general commotion, it was impossible to keep a close check on everyone.

For example: When the bottle smashed against the closet in the bedroom everyone was moving from that room toward the living room. No one saw the bottle in the air and it would have been a simple matter for someone to toss it behind him unobserved.

I do not say that is what happened, I say only that is what could have happened.

Are unnatural forces at work in the Lincoln house?

The Lincolns insist they are.

You've heard the evidence. What is your decision?

—*Raymond V. Megher, FATE contributing writer*

In Indianapolis, Indiana

Bottles smashed, tempers flashed, ashtrays shattered, and police arrested one of the principals for creating a disturbance. But when it was all over one fact remained—America's latest poltergeist case was still unexplained.

The uproar began in Indianapolis on Sunday night, March 11, 1962, a few minutes past 10:00 p.m., according to 32-year-old Mrs. Renate Beck. Mrs. Beck, a divorcee and her widowed mother, Mrs. Lina Gemmecke, 61, and Mrs. Beck's 13-year-old daughter, Linda, all live together in a huge two-story house at 2910 North Delaware St., in Indianapolis. There had been nothing unusual about the day for them until 10:37 p.m. when they heard a resounding crash upstairs.

"For a moment," said Mrs. Beck, "I thought it must have been burglars who had slipped upstairs while the three of us were all in the downstairs kitchen. There's been a lot of burglary in this city lately and that was the first thing I thought of. But when we went upstairs to look, we found that a piece of crystal that we had brought from Germany was lying on the floor about four feet from the bookcase where I had kept it—and the crystal was broken to pieces. I don't see how it got off that bookcase in the first place—nor how it landed four feet away."

The disturbed trio had little time to ponder that problem before they found themselves faced with another.

About 45 minutes after they heard the crystal smash to the bedroom floor, a heavy ashtray was flung violently against the wall of a downstairs room. Half an hour later, still another piece of crystal was broken while the three women were all huddled fearfully in the kitchen.

By midnight this series of events was too much for the ladies, and they moved to a hotel to spend the night there, unharried by the sound of breaking glass.

Although they could escape the sound of shattering crockery, it is possible that they could not evade the sounds of their own family strife. Here is an introduction to the members of the family:

The mother is Renate Beck, 32, divorced wife of a former U.S. Embassy officer whom she married in her native Vienna. Mrs. Beck is well educated and speaks English fluently, although with an accent. Presently she is not talking at all, however, on advice of her attorney. "Already too much trouble," she says.

The daughter is Linda Beck, 13. Shy and nervous, she is uncommunicative when the subject of the strange doings of the "poltergeist" is mentioned.

The grandmother is Mrs. Lina Gemmecke, 61, mother of Mrs. Beck. The moderately well-to-do widow of a newspaper publisher in Kassel, Germany, she came here three years ago after the death of her husband. Friends and neighbors tell me this has not been a tranquil or happy relationship at times, they say, it has been quite noisy and seemingly unpleasant for those directly involved.

The fourth and fifth members of the cast are Mr. and Mrs. Emil Noseda, friends of the Beck family. Noseda, 64, is a respected Indianapolis businessman who for many years operated the Sheffield Inn, one of the city's best-known hostelries. When the phenomena began at Mrs. Beck's home, she made two telephone calls—to Mr. Noseda and to the police—in that order.

Mr. and Mrs. Noseda are very important to our investigation because they are the only credible witnesses willing to go on record with a report of phenomena they have personally observed. The Nosedas are, however, not the only reliable observers who have probed the Indianapolis situation. Dr. William G. Roll, project director of the Psychical Research Foundation, Durham, North Carolina, lived in the Beck home with the family from

March 16 to 22. His reports, unfortunately, will not be made public immediately.

Until this article appears in *FATE*, the public's knowledge of the Indianapolis poltergeist will have been limited to newspaper stories based on police reports. I am going to recapitulate those police reports for you, but I give you this warning—the police reports vary dramatically from the eyewitness report made to me by Emil Noseda.

The Indianapolis police first entered the case on the second day. After a restful night at the hotel, the three women had gone home about 1:30 Monday afternoon. They found nothing amiss, but within 30 minutes of their arrival, glass was breaking again, upstairs and downstairs. The three women ran from room to room to find bowls and vases broken. When Mrs. Gemmecke arose from her chair in the kitchen and opened the door of the refrigerator, a coffee cup that had been lying in the sink across the room smashed against the wall above the chair she had just left.

Bewildered and badly frightened now, the women called police. Sergeant John L. Mullin came on the double quick. He investigated, found three nervous women, and a house littered with broken glass and crockery. Sergeant Mullin ventured the opinion that the damage had somehow been done either by a hi-fi record player or some sort of pellet gun. Both hypotheses had to be discarded. The house contained only one small record player, which was not plugged in and had not been used for weeks. And since the storm windows were all intact, the pellet gun idea was untenable.

Patrolman Ray Patton was present Monday night when the silence was broken by the sound of something falling in Linda's bedroom. He found a green glass figurine of a swan, broken in several pieces, lying in the center of the room.

Other police officers soon arrived, bringing high frequency sound gear. By the time they got there, the house was surrounded by hundreds of the curious. Other police had to be dispatched to keep the street open for traffic.

The listening gear detected nothing out of the ordinary and was removed from the premises. During the time that the gear was in use, and while the several officers were probing and prodding and postulating, there was no recurrence of the phenomena. Mrs. Beck noticed that her valise, containing $125 in the operating fund of the small restaurant she recently had opened near her home, had vanished.

Police and reporters all scoured the house for some trace of the valise. They came up empty-handed.

Now police found themselves with a new angle of this strange case. Bites—or punctures—began to appear on the hands and arms of the girl, her mother, and her grandmother. In each case ,the "bites" consisted of three tiny punctures, like those made by a bat, according to one police statement. But there were no bats flying around Indiana in midwinter, not even in a house where glasses and fishbowls, were flying.

One of the most baffling aspects of the Beck case in Indianapolis was that which occurred about 8:30 Monday night, March 12, shortly after Patrolman Ray Patton arrived as an observer. He accompanied the women on a tour of the house, which was still littered with broken glass and pottery. Mrs. Beck showed him a smashed mirror heaped on the floor where it had fallen after being knocked from the wall by a heavy ashtray, which Mrs. Beck said had sailed from her night table and into the mirror. She then showed the officer a set of three matched glasses. There had been six of them only 48 hours before, but something or someone had broken three over the weekend. For safekeeping, Mrs. Beck explained to Officer Patton, she was keeping the remaining three glasses under her hat on the dresser in her room. That's where they were when Patton last saw them together.

As the officer went through the hall one of the glasses that had been hidden under the hat struck him in the back and broke into several pieces. A moment later came the sound of more breaking glass. Patton ran back into Mrs. Beck's room and found another glass broken on the floor. He raised the hat where the three glasses had been concealed—only one remained.

When the phenomena subsided, the house on North Delaware was littered with fragments of mirrors, feathers from torn pillows, broken pottery, and dented walls and woodwork where the violently thrown objects had struck. Mrs. Beck, her mother and 13-year-old Linda began cleaning up.

But the house at 2910 Delaware St. was still not out of the news!

The missing valise returned, minus part of the money. Mrs. Beck told police that her mother had found the valise, after she felt it nudging her leg. In it, only $35 remained of the $125 it had contained when it disappeared.

The money was still unaccounted for on the night of March 25, exactly two weeks after the glassware first began to fly at the Beck home.

On March 26 police were again called to the house at 2910 Delaware "to investigate a lady." The call was evidently placed by one of the neighbors. The officer found Mrs. Gemmecke lying on the floor, apparently only semiconscious. As he paused on the landing where the stairway makes a turn, the policeman said that he saw Mrs. Gemmecke throw a heavy smoking tray against the wall and saw her upset a piano bench. He arrested her as a disorderly person.

Mrs. Beck said that her mother, a diabetic, was suffering from shock and needed medical care. She was taken first to the hospital, then after having been examined, was sent on to the city jail for the night.

Next day in court the judge proposed to hold her for a mental examination but agreed to dismiss the case if Mrs. Gemmecke returned to Germany within 10 days, as the court was told she proposed to do. She was released on bond in the custody of Mrs. Beck.

Newspapers immediately expressed the belief that the poltergeist activity at the Beck household could all be explained by the very physical actions of Mrs. Gemmecke.

The papers were aided in reaching their conclusions by some fascinating research conducted by Lt. Francis J. Dux of the Indianapolis police. Lt. Dux reported to the papers that he had "...tried to get the spirits to come out and play, but they wouldn't."

It appears that Lieutenant Dux sat everybody down in a room at the Beck house for a whole hour and a half. Nothing happened, he said, and he thereupon announced his conclusion that the phenomena happen only when one member of the household is out of sight and away from the others.

This charge, based on 90 minutes of observation, is briskly and thoroughly answered by Emil Noseda. Mr. Noseda bases his position on the fact that he was present, virtually day and night, for the entire 16 days of the occurrences. It is worth noting that the newspapers stopped reporting on the case after the sixth day. This may be in keeping with the conventional attitude toward such matters: "If you can't explain it—ignore it!"

Noseda's account of the phenomena, obtained from his friends at the house and from his own personal observations, differs from that hastily concocted and published in the Indianapolis papers.

He says that the activity began on the night of March 10, not with the breaking of a piece of crystal upstairs, but with the sudden and noisy I movement of a heavy glass beer mug which left its position on the kitchen sink and fell behind a flower pot. Both women were in the kitchen at the time. Neither of them was within reach of the mug when it moved, says Noseda.

A few minutes later, the crystal broke upstairs, while the three members of the household were downstairs. This second event prompted Mrs. Beck's calls to Noseda and the police.

Mr. Noseda says that the phenomena developed selectively: First, only glassware was affected; then the activity was transferred to chinaware. When most of the chinaware in the house had been reduced to bits, brushes, cutlery and glass jars came in for attention. Finally, he says, furniture began moving about, often times violently.

"While all of us, including my wife, were sitting in the living room," said Mr. Noseda. "A pinup lamp fell off the wall several times. I got up and drove a larger nail in the wall. Pretty soon the lamp came down again when nobody was near it. This time it broke."

"Could any of the persons in the house at that time have induced the actions of the lamp?" I asked.

"They could not. We were all sitting right there together. Nobody was within reach of the lamp. Nobody touched it. And we were all sitting in that same room together when we heard a racket in the kitchen. We went out there and found three steak knives lying on the floor in the form of a cross. They had been in a drawer about three feet from where we found them. We put them back into the drawer and all of us went back into the front room. A few minutes later, we heard the sound in the kitchen again. The knives were back out of the drawer, back on the kitchen floor in the form of a cross again. I have never seen anything like it—never!"

Newsmen mentioned that the women had complained of suffering tiny bites of some sort. Mr. Noseda says of such bites, "Yes. I saw them and so did many other persons who were present. One day, Mrs. Gemmecke was sitting on the couch and all of us were discussing the case and the damage that had been done. Suddenly Mrs. Gemmecke grabbed her throat and gasped, "They're choking me!" A policeman and I grabbed her hands and pulled them down. On the lady's throat were two sets of tiny punctures. They looked like tiny teeth marks jabbed in the form of a little triangle—on each side of her throat. They did not bleed and were given no medical attention.

"Altogether," says Mr. Noseda, "Mrs. Gemmecke was bitten nine times and Mrs. Beck was bitten twice. The flesh around the bites, or punctures, turned black and blue. But the women said the injuries caused no pain and they had no after effects."

Mr. Noseda says that he sent an eight-page airmail letter describing the weird activities to his sister in Switzerland, who he describes as a very devout woman.

"She got my letter on March 25 and took it up with her parish priest. Next morning he and my sister and several other members of that parish held a lengthy prayer session, at which they repeatedly asked that the Becks be delivered from this trouble. We did not know about this at the time, but we did notice that the phenomena at Mrs. Beck's house stopped on March 26, just 16 days after it began. It stopped on the same day that my sister attended that prayer session in Switzerland. We wrote and thanked her and the others for what they had done."

Mr. Noseda further says, "The phenomena had stopped before the police arrested Mrs. Gemmecke. I know from what I saw and heard, and from what my wife saw and heard, that neither Mrs. Gemmecke nor anyone else in that house could have done all the things that took place. There was something else involved; some force that deliberately broke up things in other parts of the house while we were all, including Mrs. Gemmecke, seated together in one room.

"I don't know what it was or how it operated but I saw it in action and I can't explain it. I never want to go through such experiences again and neither does anyone at that house!"

What is a Poltergeist?

No one knows what a poltergeist really is, but researchers have a number of well-defined theories regarding the phenomena.

There are three theories based on the hypothesis that poltergeists are associated with living personalities:

- The poltergeist is the human psyche operating outside the body.

- Poltergeist phenomena are examples of psychokinesis—the movement of objects, or matter through mental power, at a distance.

- Poltergeist phenomena are associated with an unhappy or emotionally disturbed adolescent.

A fourth theory is that poltergeist phenomena result from forces originating in personalities no longer living. This theory harks back to the original meaning of the German word *poltergeist*: rocketing ghost.

A fifth theory, favored by some conventional psychologists, is that the poltergeist exists only in the minds of the paranoid victims.

A sixth and ever-present explanation is fraud.

—*Frank Edwards, FATE contributing writer*

GET MORE AT LLEWELLYN.COM

Visit us online to browse hundreds of our books and decks, plus sign up to receive our e-newsletters and exclusive online offers.

- **Free tarot readings • Spell-a-Day • Moon phases**
- **Recipes, spells, and tips • Blogs • Encyclopedia**
- **Author interviews, articles, and upcoming events**

GET SOCIAL WITH LLEWELLYN

 **Find us on Facebook**

www.Facebook.com/LlewellynBooks

Follow us on

www.Twitter.com/Llewellynbooks

GET BOOKS AT LLEWELLYN

LLEWELLYN ORDERING INFORMATION

Order online: Visit our website at www.llewellyn.com to select your books and place an order on our secure server.

Order by phone:
- Call toll free within the U.S. at 1-877-NEW-WRLD (1-877-639-9753)
- Call toll free within Canada at 1-866-NEW-WRLD (1-866-639-9753)
- We accept VISA, MasterCard, and American Express

Order by mail:
Send the full price of your order (MN residents add 6.875% sales tax) in U.S. funds, plus postage and handling to: Llewellyn Worldwide, 2143 Wooddale Drive Woodbury, MN 55125-2989

POSTAGE AND HANDLING

STANDARD (U.S. & Canada):
(Please allow 12 business days)
$25.00 and under, add $4.00.
$25.01 and over, FREE SHIPPING.

INTERNATIONAL ORDERS (airmail only):
$16.00 for one book, plus $3.00 for each additional book.

Visit us online for more shipping options. Prices subject to change.

FREE CATALOG!

To order, call
1-877-
NEW-WRLD
ext. 8236
or visit our
website